Now We Heal
An Anthology of Hope

Editors

Jean Sheldon & Dr. Veronica Esagui

Wellworth Publishing

Now We Heal
An Anthology of Hope

ISBN: 978-0-9838136-6-8

Copyright Acknowledgements

Foreword © 2021 Jean Sheldon and Veronica Esagui

Healing Our Relationship with Our More-than-Human Community © 2021 Laurel Eloise Ladwig

The Salad Days of Summer © 2021 Judy Fleagle

Hymn for Healing and *imagine* © 2021 RC deWinter

Thriving in Any Crisis © 2021 Esther Halvorson-Hill

Imagining Our Best Selves © 2021 Veronica Esagui

Thinking of the Days That Are No More © 2021 Pat Fuller

Seasoned by Fire and *Uncorked!* © 2021 Joan Maiers

And Then There Were Ten © 2021 Judy Stone

Healing Through the Darkness © 2021 V. Falcón Vázquez

What My Daughter Knows and *I Went to Bed with an Unfinished Poem in My Mouth* © 2021 Marilyn Johnston

"What Mahler Tells Me" © 2021 John C. Fraraccio

Living in a Balanced World © 2021 Carolyn Clarke

Nobody Knows You © 2021 Jean Sheldon

The Gift, Pandemic Musings and *Healing Trauma* © 2021 Rosalyn Kliot

Writing to Wes © 2021 Lori L. Lake

Now We Know: Healing the World © 2021 Donna Reynolds

The Healing © 2021 Rena Robinett

WE. RISE. and *Avalanche* © 2021 Kim Conrad

We All Deserve Better © 2021 Keith Manuel

Wellworth Publishing
Oregon, USA

Dedicated to
Ruth Bader-Ginsberg
Fight for the things that you care about, but do it in a way that will lead others to join you

The Notorious RBG

Contents

Foreword

One sunny day, pre-COVID-19, while walking in my neighborhood, I saw a group of young people in the local park playing soccer. A break was in order, so I found a patch of grass and took a seat to watch. Peppering the sidelines were a variety of onlookers, mostly parents and siblings I'd guessed, but there was also a young boy from the neighborhood who was there with what seemed a single intent—to cheer. He didn't cheer for one side or the other, he simply cheered. He ran up and down the sidelines with the players and when anyone scored or made a great play, he cheered. His behavior never wavered, even lasting for several enthusiastic minutes after the final whistle. And along with his cheers came laughter. He laughed and cheered, cheered and laughed. It was puzzling at first, but as my mind and heart opened, I realized his behavior was not a misguided youthful response—he had figured out a far more important truth. While most attendees supported one side or the other and enjoyed only part of the game, he had found a way to appreciate every moment. With no investment in a winner, every success was reason to celebrate. How about that as a path to joyous and fulfilled living?

Our search for reasons to celebrate and be joyful in light of recent events has been challenging. We face change and disruptions that were unimaginable only a short time ago. EVERYONE is affected, which weighs heavily on our collective consciousness. In June of 2020, during a particularly discouraging stretch, the thought occurred that although I couldn't change what life was offering, I could change my focus. I began to search online for new voices, new faces, and new ideas on how to move forward in our present difficulties. It was stirring to find the internet alive with people and organizations promoting positive ways of being, and offering solid ideas for change and growth. One thought, repeated often in cyberspace, finally caught my attention—*be the change*. It was time to stop looking for others to give me hope, and be a part of bringing hope to the forefront. But honestly, I wasn't sure what I could do. After some effort reviving "lockdown" brain cells from their stupor, I considered that I could use my skills as a writer and publisher to share the stories others had to offer. A collection focused on hope and healing had potential because, judging by responses on social media, the world was starved for both.

My first outreach was to friend and fellow author, Dr. Veronica Esagui, who was enthusiastic about the idea and anxious to help. We shared our intentions with friends and family, posted our call to authors on social media and other venues and waited for a response.

Our request was for articles that showed who we are without hate, anger or rage. Stories that highlighted compassion and healing to move us forward and perhaps confront the painfully unresolved issues in our society that have become clear. We asked for stories that remind us of our boundless inner strength and the gifts we can offer because of it. We welcomed all genre, and, remarkably, many were submitted!

What will you find in this collection? One of our authors introduces you to an intergalactic granny who joins with protestors to save their planet. Another author, who lost loved ones to heart disease, shares her experience and knowledge on the advantages of a plant-based diet. From another, readers can explore an informative and enlightening introduction to the music of Gustav Mahler. Or perhaps you'll find comfort in what an octogenarian shares about how her own life lessons enable her to thrive in this time of global pandemic. There are stories of a healing present and a healing future. Stories of resilience and hope. Stories that suggest ways to save the planet and the animals with which we share it. And if those aren't enough to entice you, several poets share their inspirations in ways that only poets can.

With the uniqueness of our times in the forefront, I was aware that it took a good deal of inner fortitude to focus and write for this anthology. Because of that, I am doubly grateful to those who contributed. Thank you! Thank you also to Catherine and Jude for positive feedback and support during the mulling stages and beyond.

My natural optimism has been tested in these complicated times, but in compiling this anthology, I was reminded that giving in to darkness never serves anyone well. I'm glad to have had the opportunity to read and share the caring and healing words of our contributors. In the end, I guess I did look to others to find hope, but perhaps finding hope in each other is the real lesson after all. My hope is that you will find yours. And if you need me, I'll be on the sidelines, laughing and cheering your every goal, your every success and your every effort.

Jean

I feel privileged and honored that Jean Sheldon, publisher and creator of this book, asked me to join as co-editor. Her insightful enthusiasm, and the amazing heartfelt contributions by these many talented authors has created what I believe was Jean's original intent, a book that opens our hearts and brings hope, healing and the prospect of a better future for everyone.

Veronica Esagui

The sole purpose of human existence is to kindle a light in the darkness of mere being.

~Carl Jung

Healing Our Relationship with Our More-than-Human Community

Laurel Eloise Ladwig

In this time of global change, we have the challenge and opportunity to recognize our entanglement with the natural world and find ways of transforming our relationship into one based on reciprocity and respect. Given that humans are the primary agent of change on the planet, we have to work to create a world where both human and more-than-human community members can thrive. Recognizing our membership in the multispecies community and learning to share habitat with all our wild neighbors is a good place to start.

In reshaping our thinking about dandelions or other so-called

*weeds, we might reshape our
entire relationship with
the living world.*

~Robin Wall Kimmerer

Our backyards can be a window into our wondrously complex natural world, filled with extraordinary interactions and interdependencies. A common refrain is that everything is connected to everything but it is countless specific relationships that make this true—from aphids and hummingbirds to bagworms and Bushtits. What some call pests and weeds are of vital importance to other members of our community. Dandelions are often the first source of nectar for pollinators in early spring. Aphids on roses provide protein for growing hummingbird babies. Dead branches on trees provide food, shelter, and perching spots for myriad species. Leaf litter retains moisture and creates foraging habitat for sparrows. Rodents are food for owls and other raptors. Bagworm cocoons are full of silk that Bushtits harvest for building soft and strong shelter for their nestlings. (Anything that helps to bring more baby Bushtits into the world is worth celebrating.)

I first noticed the Bushtit/bagworm relationship this April when a Bushtit couple were in our yard hour after hour, day after day, collecting nesting material. I was so excited that they might be nesting in our yard, but it takes a community to raise a cloud of Bushtits. Our neighbors' dense conifer provided the perfect sheltered environment for their sock-like nest. Our yard supplied mouthful after mouthful of nesting material. Countless nearby shrubs and trees had insects that fed the growing family. Our Vitex shrub served as an afternoon napping and snacking spot for multiple families' fledglings. The youngsters even used our empty peanut feeder to cuddle together and swing.

> *Skill in living, awareness of belonging to the world, delight in being part of the world, always tends to involve knowing our kinship as animals with animals.*
>
> ~Ursula K. Le Guin

Robin Wall Kimmerer, author of "Braiding Sweetgrass", says that "we need not only to heal the land but also to heal our relationship to land" and that restoring habitat can do both. My master's research found that those who consider our wild neighbors to be kin are most willing to take action to manage their yards in ways that benefit wildlife. Creating habitat in our yards is an opportunity to put our love, care, reverence, and respect into practice.

Sharing space with wildlife in our yards and communities creates opportunities for learning about the lives of our neighbors and observing the relationships that story our living world. Nature's voice is expressed in action all around us. Observing and attempting to understand the ways other species live their lives is key to embracing them as members of our community and building habitat we can share. By becoming aware of their needs and making simple changes in our yards and lives we can make space for other species to flourish with us in our interdependent community.

Care obliges us to constant fostering...a world's degree of livability might well depend on the caring accomplished within it.

~Maria Puig de la Bellacasa

Sharing space with our resident and migratory wildlife has never been more important. In this time of changing climate, wildlife face daunting challenges. At the backyard scale, we can share our resources and be responsive to the needs of our wild neighbors. Spending time in our yards focusing care and attention on our wild neighbors can remind us to enjoy our membership in the community of life while providing wildlife with space and resources for adapting to a changing world.

Begin to learn the language of your wild neighbors. Listen for the sounds of wildlife going about their day. You may hear a conversation between goldfinches, woodpeckers tapping, a sparrow scratching for edible bits in the leaf litter, squirrels chirping a warning call, or a cloud of bushtits' high-pitched chatter as they glean tiny insects from the trees and bushes in your yard.

Sharing habitat and caring for our wild neighbors is an expression of hope for the future of our more-than-human world. Treating our fellow species as family and working in cooperation with our wild kin can help us find new ways of living within a flourishing multi-species community on a changing planet.

Laurel Ladwig is a more-than-human geographer living in Albuquerque, New Mexico. A lifelong birder and naturalist, Laurel organizes citizen science projects that encourage people to develop a relationship with the more-than-human world. ladwings@gmail.com, Instagram: ladwings iNaturalist: pbgrebe www.abqbackyardrefuge.org

The Salad Days of Summer

Judy Fleagle

Home grown, vine ripened tomatoes in summer on the coast of Oregon? Not gonna happen, unless...

...you have a real hot spot or a greenhouse. Not having a hotspot, that left a greenhouse as an option. I had wanted a greenhouse for ages, but my husband, Walt, always said, "Too expensive!" However, he had a passion for vine-ripened tomatoes. And we were both tired of seeing tomato plants in the yard filled with green tomatoes that never ripened.

So, when we saw greenhouses for sale in a grocery store parking lot in January, we stopped to take a look. We discovered that these one-piece, Fiberglas greenhouses were a whole lot cheaper than others we had looked at. But it was the brochure filled with photos of red, vine-ripened tomatoes that was the clincher. As soon as Walt said, "Well, maybe!" I whipped out the checkbook.

Two weeks later, the greenhouse arrived, a month earlier than expected. Walt, who had been diagnosed with late-stage Hodgkin's Disease a few months before, was on a regimen of chemotherapy that had severely weakened his immune system. Since ordering the greenhouse, he had developed a life-threatening infection that put him in the hospital. I spent my time there with him and not preparing a level spot for the greenhouse. So it sat tilting precariously on a slope behind the house.

The second night after its arrival, a storm hit. I got up, put my raincoat on over my nightgown and stopped in the garage to grab boots, a rope, some stakes, a mallet, and a flashlight. On a windy, slippery slope by the light of a flashlight, I threw a rope over the greenhouse and staked it. The next morning, it was quite a relief to see it still there.

Two neighbors, who had offered to help, came over the next day. We set to work with tape measure, stakes, a level, and shovels. A couple, who lived up the hill, saw what was happening and joined in with their shovels and a ball of twine.

We dug sod and roots and shoveled dirt from one place to another. It started to drizzle, but we kept at it. After three hours, we had a level spot measuring 8½ by 18 feet with the necessary six-inch trench around the perimeter.

The five of us—tired but determined—grunted and groaned the greenhouse into place. When it settled in, our cheers said it all. It took only moments to pack soil in the trench, stabilizing the structure.

The next day, I brought Walt home. He was weak and depressed, but seeing the greenhouse raised his spirits. Of course, he wanted to plant tomato seeds right then.

But it would be a while before we planted tomato seeds or anything else. A lot of work needed to be done, starting with steps from house to greenhouse. They would detour around four terraces, which had been recently constructed to hold the steepest part of the slope. Piles of dirt—left over from that project and the greenhouse leveling—would have to be moved around and leveled to make the area usable between the terraces and the greenhouse.

I shuttled between stints as Walt's nurse and my new role as excavation engineer. I dug wet, heavy blocks of soil and weeds and wheelbarrowed them away. Some loads had stumps and roots. Those were more of a challenge. Even using a pick, I ended up pulling with every ounce of strength I could muster. As with the greenhouse leveling, I moved dirt from one spot to another until the area was relatively flat and weed free.

Walt gradually gained back some strength. When he could operate a chainsaw, we bought railroad ties for the steps. We had them loaded onto the back of our flatbed truck, where Walt could cut them. Even though I couldn't carry them, I end-over-ended them downhill.

Before I could set the ties in place, I had to remove more sod. And because each spot had to be level, it took forever to place 10 half-ties as steps around the terraces. Then I placed four full-size ties as steps leading to a level area in front of the greenhouse.

Next, I ordered gravel. One of the green-house-helping neighbors helped me wheelbarrow load after load downhill and spread it inside the greenhouse, on the newly leveled area, and between the new steps. I thought wet sod was heavy. It doesn't compare to gravel!

For weeks, my back had been letting me know what it thought of my heavy-duty exertions. But the aches and pains were worth it when Walt walked down to the greenhouse the first time, smiled, and said, "Looks, damn good!"

With visions of vine-ripened tomatoes dancing in his head, he worked short spurts between chemo cycles. He was able to put together two pre-cut, 15-foot-long benches that came with the greenhouse. He mounted hangers above the benches and built a table with shelves and a stand for grow lights.

While he was busy in the greenhouse, I worked the sandy loam soil outside in the lower two terraces with lime, organic material, and fertilizer.

In the greenhouse, we put planter mix in the four deep trays that came with the greenhouse. They fit perfectly into one bench along one side. Then we covered the other bench with a metal mesh (hardware cloth) that could support planter boxes and pots. For water and electricity, we ran a hose and a long, heavy-duty extension cord from the house.

At last, we were ready to plant. The seeds sprouted quickly with the aid of heating coils. Then we put them under grow lights that extended their growing time each day. We watched the seedlings turn green and grow straight and sturdy in the diffused light of the greenhouse. We cheered them on each step of the way. As they became robust little plants, they were transplanted outside or elsewhere in the greenhouse.

After planting, came the watering, weeding, and fertilizing. Somehow, these chores just didn't seem like work.

In July, our dream came true, as we picked our first delicious, vine-ripened tomatoes. By then, we had a garden and greenhouse full of vegetables with enough left over to share with our wonderful, supportive neighbors. By August, Walt's chemo was over. He was in remission. And I had learned that I could accomplish almost anything, if I put my mind to it. We had, indeed, earned the right to enjoy the salad days of summer.

Judy Fleagle taught first and second grades in California for 22 years. She and her late husband moved to Florence, Oregon in 1985 where she became an editor/staff writer at Oregon Coast and Northwest Travel magazines for 21 years. Since 2009, she has embarked on a third career. She has authored five books: *Crossings: McCullough's Coastal Bridges*, *The Crossings Guide to Oregon's Coastal Spans*, *Around Florence (history 1876-present)*, *Devil Cat and Other Colorful Animals I Have Known* (five stories about rescue animals that became great pets), and *The Oregon Coast Guide to the UNEXPECTED that which is odd, unusual or quirky!!!* To order books online go to crossingsauthor.com/books

Hymn for Healing

RC deWinter

Someday we're going to be out in the streets
laughing and singing and dancing again,
free of the lies, the oppression, deceits,
We'll have a new chance to be human then.

Someday the color of skin will not be
a judgment of worthiness, humanity.
And be you a he or be you a she,
gender will no longer be vanity.

Someday we'll learn how to look past the
    face,
to see beyond what is an envelope.
Compassion and tolerance we will embrace,
to know we're part of a kaleidoscope.

All blood bleeds red when you open a vein,
take off the blinders, it's easy to see
in laughter and tears, in joy and in pain,
just look at each other: I'm you, you're me.

imagine
© 2021 RC deWinter

when night became day the clock stopped
we were left fumbling in the indifference
of a lightless timeless existence
intuition our only guide

barriers fell as we encountered each other
with no preconceived prejudices
to color our perception of strangers
that level playing field changed everything

oh the usual hatreds and greed surfaced
on occasion but eventually were drowned
in the glue of cooperation because
no one could survive as an island

even as i lived it i knew it was a dream
a virtual vacation from the dog eat dog of
an overpopulated underresourced planet
        where
the clock never stops and money always wins
but when i woke wrapped in a lightness
i'd lost long ago i was smiling a miracle in itself

and with lennon singing in my head
set about to make night day

RC deWinter writes in several genres with a focus on poetry. She is also a digital artist and sometimes chanteuse. Her only claim to fame is a decent Twitter following. RC deWinter's poetry is widely anthologized, notably in *New York City Haiku* (Universe/NY Times/Rizzoli, 2/2017), *Nature In The Now* (Tiny Seed Press, 8/2019), *Coffin Bell Two* (2/2020), *Other Worldly Women Press 2020 Summer Anthology: a Headrest for Your Soul* (6/2020), in print in *2River, Adelaide, Event, Genre Urban Arts, Gravitas, Kansas City Voices, Meat For Tea: The Valley Review, the minnesota review, Night Picnic Journal, Prairie Schooner, Southword*, among others and appears in numerous online literary journals.

Thriving in Any Crisis

Esther Halvorson-Hill

People have been asking me how I have been doing during the COVID-19 epidemic, and I have answered, "I seem to be thriving." How can that be? I am an almost 80-year-old woman living alone.

I remember my mother quoting this Bible verse to me when I was a child and I have used it as a guide during most of my long life.

Fix your thoughts on what is true and good and right.

Think about things that are pure and lovely.

Dwell on the fine, good things in others.

Think about all you can praise God for and be glad about.

Philippians 4:8 The Living Bible Paraphrased

I confess that I have not always remembered the exact wording, but I have embraced the gist of it. My life has mostly been positive as a result. I do not seem to focus on things or events that are negative.

When I look back on the past 6 months, I can identify these concepts that have been helpful for me.

LOOK for BEAUTY

I found that the beauty of nature thrilled me and gave me peace. With so many people confined to their homes, it seemed like nature started some healing. I was encouraged by reports of wild animals becoming freer to roam around Yosemite National Park or even in the deserted streets of some cities. I read reports of endangered turtle species returning to the empty beaches to lay their eggs. There were many such reports. Photographs of places devoid of crowds looked especially lovely.

On social media, beautiful scenes were shared. Members of Facebook from across the world, started a project where they shared views from their porches or windows. This showcased the wonderful beauty and variety in our world. I would look forward each day to see what was posted. It brought people from many countries together and kept the natural beauty of our planet in our thoughts.

Also, on social media, people began sharing pictures of flowers they had received or picked, pictures of beauty they had seen on their travels, or even homey things such as newly baked bread or special meals.

LOOK for JOY

I found joy in the quiet of my home, in reading a good novel, in watching birds at my outdoor feeder. My pet lovebirds that were laying eggs and producing new baby birds gave me joy.

I found joy when people would contact me to see if I was doing all right; show up (masked) with a gift at my door, or offer to get groceries for me.

I found joy when my super busy family now had time to contact me more often.

I found joy from my church and personal calls from my minister.

Music has always brought me joy. Although I was not able to perform with fellow musicians, many were performing virtually from their homes.

KEEP HEALTHY

It was serendipitous that I had just started a Nutrisystem diet right before the COVID-19 epidemic started. Food was delivered right to my door, so I did not have to do much grocery shopping.

I was better nourished on a more balanced diet. I also found that eating my meals at home made my Condo seem much more like home.

I tend to eat most meals out at local restaurants and would have missed doing this. While being quarantined, I knew I could not have eaten out anyway.

Exercise continued to be important to me. My twice weekly personal trainer sessions continued with Zoom. My Fitbit tracking watch gave my days structure that might have otherwise been missing. It prompted me to get in 250 steps an hour and keep moving. That kept me conscious of time passing and kept me from just zoning out.

BE THANKFUL for THE GIFT of TIME

I found that I had time to write. I finished a compilation of newspaper articles I had written into book form. This was very satisfying.

I found time to organize my condo. My recent move had taken place when I had not had time to thoughtfully place and organize my belongings. While on quarantine, I realized this and was able to sort and significantly downsize. I had time to organize a huge collection of paper and documents, some from 15-20 years ago. They are now organized into easily accessed folders with a good index. I had been having trouble finding things. This process helped immensely.

My love of reading really helped expand my limited quarantine space into adventures in other countries and times. I am blessed with a very vivid imagination. I had more time to read.

Lately I have discovered Vacation Adventure computer games that with my imagination take me on camping trips or luxury cruises. I could not figure out why I felt so relaxed and happy after playing these "hidden object" games. I think that in my imagination, I am going on these trips. I am currently visiting Egypt.

SOCIALIZE VIRTUALLY

I am so appreciative of social media such as Facebook. When not able to get out and socialize, I began to really value my virtual community composed of people known in high school, college, work life, organizations, and my local community. This virtual community expanded during the quarantine to include people from other countries.

How often does one get to see Andrea Bocelli in his home encouraging his daughter to play the piano? I watched the video and listened when she mastered the piece and he added his glorious tenor voice. This was such an intimate glimpse of a famous talent. I was also thrilled to experience him singing alone in a great Cathedral in Italy on Easter morning. If I had not been quarantined, I would have been busy with Easter festivities and would have missed this.

Spiritual and church family can be accessible by phone or texting. Phone calls by other church members and the minister can be wonderful.

Getting one's mind off oneself and onto others is especially important. Texting and offering encouragement to those who are living alone is a blessing to them and to yourself.

BE CREATIVE: Don't Lose Your Inner Child

The current situation has forced us to be creative and find new ways of doing things.

Education is being reinvented. I was involved early on in distance education when I was teaching nursing leadership at Oregon Health Sciences University, so recent changes seem natural and exciting.

Music has always been and continues to be important to me. I do miss playing with local groups and performing, however. I am excited to see musicians who have been virtually playing and sharing their music.

Choirs have been adapting. Virtual choirs with individual singers being taped singing in their own homes and then joined have been quite successful. One local church has posting organ and piano music daily.

Churches have utilized YouTube to produce weekly services. Some have even begun to reach a larger number of listeners. I appreciate being able to attend a church service whenever I wish and sometimes even in PJs.

Entertainment is being reinvented. Television programs have had to adapt suddenly to lack of large audiences and social distancing. We have seen, and are seeing, some highly creative programing.

One must be comfortable with and enjoy their own company to thrive when living alone during a quarantine. Thank goodness I have this trait.

What my life will be like post COVID-19 is hard to know, but it will be different. In a good way, I think. I see this time as an opportunity instead of a loss. I am reminded of a lotus flower growing out of the mud. Something good can result if one remains positive.

I have been temporarily released from old community responsibilities such as doing the monthly newsletter for a local organization. I enjoyed doing it at the time, but now I find it a relief not having the responsibility, and will not be doing that in the future.

Though almost 80 I feel very much younger. I think it is time to reinvent myself for this last phase of my life. This quarantine has provided a time for introspection. It is exciting to contemplate how this last phase might look.

Esther Halvorson-Hill is a retired Associate Professor of Nursing. During her long career as a nurse she held the positions of staff nurse, Senior Clinical Nurse, Charge Nurse, Floor Manager, Inservice Director, and Director of Nursing. After retirement she became a professional musician, both vocal and flute. Esther graduated from Stanford University in 1963 and received graduate degrees from Oregon Health Sciences University and Portland State University. She has published articles in *Oasis Journal 2015* and *Oasis Journal 2016.* She is a member of the Jottings Group in Lake Oswego, OR and has published many articles in the *Lake Oswego Review.* This year, she has written *Musings,* a compilation of her 24 newspaper articles.

Imagining Our Best Selves

Veronica Esagui

When the Berlin wall came down in 1989, I excitedly told others that such an event only proved that we were closer to achieving peace on Earth. They called me a dreamer, and some even laughed, but I wasn't then, and am still not ashamed of dreaming. I like to imagine a world without hunger, a world where compassion is practiced by everyone without a second thought. I believe kindness is an inborn quality that we all possess, and I like to imagine how we can use it to make the world a better place.

I dream of a world where disease no longer exists, because there is no profit to be made from the sick. I imagine a world where the young listen to their elders and the cumulative knowledge of the ages is passed on. I'm even imagining the possibility that those who are the beacons of humanity will never die. Why not? It's my dream. I can imagine anything I want. I can imagine that the earth will no longer be exploited, but instead treated as a holistic entity for which we are all responsible. I can imagine an end to the extinction of all species, and that terrorism is non-existent; that illiteracy and poverty are a thing of the past. I can imagine that our knowledge enables us to visit other planets, and we are delighted to learn that we are not alone and can carry the gift of love across the Universe, because we know there is more than enough to share.

> *We are what we think. All that*
> *we are arises with our*
> *thoughts. With our thoughts*
> *we make the world.*
> ~Buddha

Though they may not say it, I am absolutely certain that many feel as I do. This ongoing dream for equality has been alive and evolving since the beginning of time. Some say it will never happen, but I know it will. It's just a question of when the whole of humanity shares the same vision.

We hold these truths to be self-evident, that all men are created equal, that they are endowed by their Creator with certain unalienable Rights, that among these are Life, Liberty and the pursuit of Happiness.

United States Declaration of Independence
July 4, 1776

One hundred and eighty-seven years after the creation of that document, many African Americans still faced widespread discrimination —politically, socially, and economically. A key moment in U.S. history came about on August 28, 1963 when American civil rights activist Dr. Martin Luther King Jr, dared to bring his dream into reality. Along with 250,000 supporters he led the March for Jobs and Freedom on Washington to call for civil and economic rights and an end to racism in the US. His "I Have a Dream" speech was never forgotten and as a result of the March, the Civil Rights Act of 1964 was passed to bring an end to segregation in public places and employment discrimination on the basis of race, color, religion, sex or national origin. Dr. King Jr. fought for justice in the United States and, across the globe, Nelson Mandela led the movement to end apartheid in South Africa. He became the first Black president of South Africa and in 1993 won the Nobel Peace Prize.

Sadly, 244 years after the Declaration of Independence came into existence, we are still divided, but in my heart, I know there is hope. Every day we see people join together to resist those who try to divide humanity using religion, race, political views, sexual orientation and more, and with each resistance they move us forward. Though it may not always feel like it, they are making a difference. The year 2020 marked the first time ever that people across the globe voiced their dream for peace and unity. The COVID-19 world pandemic has done its best to keep us apart, but I feel that we are now closer to our neighbors around the world than we have ever been.

Change will not come if we wait for some other person or some other time. We are the ones we've been waiting for. We are the change that we seek.

~Barack Obama

Martin Niemöller, (1892-1984) a prominent Lutheran pastor in Germany said:

> First they came for the socialists,
>   and I did not speak out—Because
>   I was not a socialist.
> Then they came for the trade union-
>   ists, and I did not speak out—Be-
>   cause I was not a trade unionist.
> Then they came for the Jews, and I
>   did not speak out—Because I was
>   not a Jew.
> Then they came for me—and there
>   was no one left to speak for me.

Niemöller spent the last seven years of Nazi rule as a prisoner in a concentration camp.

As we move forward, I want to do my part to help us heal. I will take time to reflect, to look inward, and then reach out.

Dr. Veronica Esagui, is the author of critically acclaimed *The Scoliosis Self-Help Resource Book* in English and Japanese. As a motivational guest speaker on board the Princess Cruises, she traveled to Panama Canal in 2017, Asia in 2018, and South America in 2020. Publisher, playwright and poet she is also the author of *Veronica's Diary* sequels: *The Journey of Innocence, Braving a New World, Awakening the Woman Within, Angels Among Us* and *The Gift*. Her next book, *The Tue Story of the Mary Celeste,* historical fiction, is soon to be released. www.veronicaesagui.com

Thinking of the Days That Are No More

Pat Fuller

Sunday's were the most difficult. I'd look across the yard and see the children racing each other to get to my house. But they are gone. No more treks to Grandma's. I try not to cry, but it's like biting down on a sore tooth. I can't help myself. Oh, the days that are no more! Why didn't I appreciate it more?

I'll ask that until I die.

None of us can go back to what was. We can only learn from the experience and try to do better.

In March of 2019, my world was turned upside down. My daughter-in-law, who'd been born and raised on an Indian Reservation, announced that she and my son and the grandchildren were moving to New Mexico. Ever since she'd left as a young woman, Anna had dreamt of returning and helping her people. Now, she had been offered a position with the Tribe. It was the opportunity she'd always wanted. How was I to put impediments in her way? I prayed for the highest good of all concerned. Everything fell into place and by June they were gone.

I felt abandoned! It was like a death as far as my grieving was concerned. Our former life died the day they pulled away with their car towed behind a U-Haul truck. As I cycled through the stages of grieving, I decided that we could go to see them. So we planned a trip. It was so good and healing that we planned another for a few months later. That trip, too, helped with the healing.

Then, winter came. And the coronavirus came to our country.

Gradually, everything began to change.

As more of us realized the implications, we all began cycling through the stages of grieving. Grieving for our country and the lost opportunities we'd missed to unite and fight against the virus.

Our next trip to New Mexico was cancelled. Life has a peculiar way of throwing curves at you to see how tough you really can become.

Through everything that has happened since they left, I have learned that gratitude is the key for me to be content. Rather than bemoan my losses, I chose to focus on what I have. And I am blessed.

The moral I guess is to appreciate what you have.

Anything can happen and everything can change in an instant.

Life is fragile, they say. Cherish each moment.

Face forward, not back. Look to the future. Smile.

Pat Fuller grew up in Central Illinois and received her B.S.Ed. From Illinois State University. Later, she received a M.A. degree from Bradley University. She is a retired school counselor and was previously a teacher who has been married for 50 years. Her husband had four children when they got married. They had three more. Family is one of her prime motivations. They have 16 grandchildren and 13 great-grandchildren. What a blessing!

Seasoned by Fire

Joan Maiers

Where late summer air hovers
about hedges and lawns,
a Bartlett pear tree stands loaded
with golden fruits, gravity-bound
in a residential section
dissected by dirt alleys.
They border the workers' cottages,
and homes—Queen Annes, faux
Victorians, or ranch style.
Polished by the sun's rays,
each fruit, teardrop-shaped,
eases onto dry grasses
tapestried across the earth
where bees drone
their exploratory caresses.

Uncorked!

Gallery visitors sidle along the floorboards,
oat-straw panels polished to a dull gloss.
They attend to views of local vineyards.
A hostess pours customary wines or sparkling
    water.
Red is first to go
for gazers intent
as sharks gliding for nutrients.
Like mascots, the women's purses snuggle in
their arms, or they lie
athwart their backs, freeing
the owners to gesture at brushstrokes
in tempera, watercolor, crude oils, mixed media.
Surgeons from the clinic next door
visit outside next to ivy-filigreed walls,
while inside, a chalky orb winks
out from the landscape titled Strawberry
    Moon,
waiting to belong to someone
for only 350 dollars.

Joan Maiers works with writers of all ages, ranging from primary grades through post-retirement years. Her work appears in collections and anthologies like *Blooming in the Shade; If I Had a Hammer--On Women and Work; Raising Our Voices*, and regional publications, such as *Green Living*

Journal, Hubbub, Fireweed, Windfall, and *Oregon English.* She is preparing her manuscript, *Specific Gravity,* for publication. After the pandemic, she will resume hosting the regional Peregrine Literary Series.

And Then There Were Ten

Judy Stone

Many years after Lee and Dorothy Stone adopted me from Chicago's St. Vincent's Orphanage in 1939, I began searching for my birth mother. I was in my mid-fifties by then, and wanted to satisfy basic curiosity about my real roots and to obtain some personal and health information. My usual answer, for example about medical requests for family history was "Unknown." My parents had both passed away by my mid-twenties and in my mid-fifties I took a class in which we were to write a paper giving as much history as we could about our heritage. In reality, I could have just as easily responded "unknown" but, instead, wrote a paper about the families of my parents, Lee and Dorothy.

Pushed to probe

In the early 1990s, I found a woman I was pretty sure was my birth mother. Armed with a phone number and a lifelong desire for answers, I made the call, and when a man answered, not knowing if anyone but her even knew of my existence, I asked to speak to Rita. When she came on the line, I mentioned my birth date and the belief that she was my mother. Her response was "Oh my child, I have prayed for you every day of your life." (There had been about 50 years' worth of them at the time). My heart was setting records in pounding speed and volume when I heard her say to the man who had answered "This is the little girl we gave up."

As it turned out, George and Rita Busse were married about three years after my birth and went on to have nine other children. In a matter of seconds, I went from never knowing a blood relation to being the oldest of ten full brothers and sisters. It is rare for adoptees to have this kind of experience—most tend to find only their mother. Upon discovering they too still lived in Chicago, I wanted to see them. The next day, a friend drove me to the other side of the city where I found my father waiting at the top of the stairs. He said "I would have known you were one of ours from the moment you got out of the car. You look just like your sister Margie." He was right! In fact, Margie and I became known as the 'bookends.'

The Adoption Triangle

Searching for birth family information was quite a challenge at that time—no search engines and very closed records. Some of the obstacles come from what is described as the adoption triangle: the adoptive parents, the birth parents and the child placed into the adoption process; and the concept that the "best interests of the child" would be uppermost in all considerations. In reality, the triangle was set up to protect the adoptive parents so they need not worry that birth parents, who were not seen in the most positive of lights, could ever show up to reclaim their child. The agencies typically examined the adoptive parents through visitations and inquiries as to their appropriateness, i.e. a good Catholic family. This was often a rather long and laborious process to determine, as much as was possible, that the placements would be good ones. This, they concluded, gave the typically "born out of wedlock" or "bastard child" a better likelihood of a good life with good people—certainly with "better" people than those who gave up a child. While this was supposedly done with the child in mind, mostly it prohibited the child from knowing anything related to their birth heritage. It was also to assure that the parent or parents who were giving up the child would never know anything about what happened to their child, keeping the adoptive parents safe from worry. Often duplicity was a part of the triangularity—the agencies or orphanages often changed information so that the names submitted to the county officials to set up certificates of birth (rather than true birth certificates) were altered with incorrect names and sometimes incorrect dates of birth.

As an aside, our certificates of birth look nothing like a true birth certificate. Prior to going into the Peace Corps, I went downtown to get a copy of my birth certificate as a necessary paper to get my passport. I waited and waited and waited as many others who came into the office received their birth certificates without wait or difficulty. After a very long period I was ushered into the office of the head of records who asked tentatively if I knew that my birth certificate was quite a different looking document. Truthfully, I said "No." Then, noticing his discomfort, I asked if that was because I had been adopted. He took a deep breath and with obvious relief said yes and gave me my certificate of birth. I thought it lovely that this man was so concerned that he might be perhaps the first person to tell me of my adoption.

The agency and orphanage personnel would assure the adoptive parents that the records would be sealed and unavailable to anyone. Priests and nuns in the Catholic orphanages lectured the birth parent not to ever attempt to find their child. This was told to Rita Busse, and as a good Catholic girl, who had done a bad thing by getting pregnant out of wedlock, when the priest told her to never, never, never try to find her child, that was what she did. That order came, no doubt, with required ample penance for her sin and tons of guilt.

The records, often altered, were sealed, and accessing any information was difficult. Adoptive parents were coached on how to handle inquiries from friends, relatives or the adoptees themselves. The adopted kids were to be told they were special because they had been chosen and wanted, whereas other kids were just born into the family. Once a neighbor called my mom and asked her to stop my brother (also adopted from the same orphanage two years before me) and I from saying that we were special because her child had come home in tears when he realized he had not been "chosen". This was one of the ways we were told to deal with our heritage and as "special kids" we tended to be really well behaved. We were often told how good we were and how wonderful our parents were to adopt us.

Abandonment is a big issue. When one starts life in an abandoned state (from the psychologist in me) there is a wound and a wonder as to when or if this might happen again. My parents were wonderful and loving and I was and am most fortunate that my early life was with them. However, the theme of abandonment has been an issue, and research suggests that there is an unrecognized fear that one might be taken back or turned in if one was not a really good kid. My mom's death when I was ten was a massive blow. The loss of a mom for any kid at ten is life-changing and tremendous, but for me as an adoptee I couldn't help but wonder if something happened to my dad—would I be taken back to the orphanage?

My parents were always a bit vague when I asked about what people often called my "real parents." They told me that they were good Catholic people (kind of insinuating that they were married) but had so little money that they wanted me to have a better home than they could afford. Many years later, when I finally saw my adoption decree, which listed only my mother, I felt shame and embarrassment to realize I was, in fact, born out of wedlock, so perhaps Dorothy and Lee were right to imply my birth parents were married. By the way, my real parents were Dorothy and Lee Stone. The people who are your parents are those who truly parented you, not the ones who made you.

I remember a woman who spoke at one of my Ph.D. classes that focused on heritage who had been an early advocate of getting records opened and unsealed because of her own experiences. She had been adopted and grown up in a Scandinavian home where her parents, siblings and other relatives were blonde and blue eyed. Donna was not, and she spoke about what an incredible feeling she had upon her first meeting with birth family members. She got off a plane in St. Louis and immediately recognized her family because they were all redheads with brown eyes matching her own.

Adoptees never know anyone who resembles them. When I first met my brother, Mike, he stood up in the restaurant where we had arranged to meet and recognized me from across the room. And after I met the first three of my siblings, I knew descriptions of my outfit were no longer necessary. It was, and sometimes, still is, weird when friends of mine can't get over how much I look like the family. It has taken me years to be able to see or recognize the resemblances myself.

The process has changed some and today it is a little easier for adoptees to find their birth parents, although it is usually only the mother. When they meet their child, they typically want to know three things: Did you have a good home? Did you turn out okay? Did you, or can you forgive me? Often, they get this information in the first meeting and then do not want to continue the relationship—the guilt, the shame, the secret, etc. The secret has been hidden for so long that many husbands who are typically not the birth father do not know that their wives had given up and child, and thus their children do not know...and the beat goes on. Many birth mothers will not agree to meet with their child so the rejection and abandonment is magnified. Scores of adoptees do not want to know and make little or no effort to find birth families.

It was incredibly hard for me to push for more time together when George and Rita pulled away after meeting with them only twice. The first meeting was incredibly warm and touching and truly wonderful, but the second meeting was stilted and they were very uncomfortable and distant. Clearly, they did not want to continue as their three questions had been answered. Several years passed, but I persevered and at one of our clandestine Christmas dinners my father, George, asked what I wanted for Christmas. This prompted Rita to elbow him and say "You know what she wants." He then said "Could you not wait until we're in our happy hunting ground?" I was being pressured to be a part of their deception to not inform my siblings yet, but could not imagine turning up in their lives after these revered (my mother was often called St. Rita) and loving parents had passed away. Imagine saying "by the way, I'm the sister you never knew about." So, after years of hopeful waiting for them to change their minds, I wrote the letter below. It had been on my mind for some time and when I sat down to write it, I simply wrote. No editing was done.

November 21, 1995

Greetings to both of you,

Guess you have been wondering why there has been such a period of silence—primarily from my end. Perhaps you are feeling relieved—it is hard to know since we haven't spoken for some months now—actually about six or so.

My difficulty lies, as you probably have guessed or surmised, in the continued need on your part to keep the silence about your 56-year-old secret. I know that you have probably only shared my emergence with Ann who is about the only one who knows about me anyway.

My story about you and my brothers and sisters has been told more times than you could imagine. You see, most people are touched by our reunion and our relationship and tell the story to their friends. A very typical response is for people to cry because they are so touched by this tale. Always there are questions and the first usually is— what are they like? And I tell them you are both terrific and wonderful.

Inevitably the next question is what was it like to meet your brothers and sisters. And then I carefully tell them of your feelings and preferences—letting mine go because they are not relevant to the decision. While almost everyone can understand your reluctance, shame/guilt, etc., they see your decision as primarily a selfish and self-protective one. And most of the time, I do as well.

These are people who range in age from teens to women in their eighties. In fact, two very special people who are both 85, as Irish and as Catholic as the days are long, have suggested that perhaps I could get a priest to help you work through this because they feel that we should all be allowed to meet each other. I have literally had to stop a few people who felt so strongly about this that they literally had planned to call a brother, such as Joe, or stop in to see Danny and tell them.

I have been very patient because I really felt that, given time, you would change your stance. I have known addresses and phone numbers of my nine siblings ever since I found your phone number. I simply do not want to wait until you both die to meet them and I feel it is unfair of you to ask me that.

I know there is concern about the in-laws but I do not need to meet them or to haven them know about me. You can ask my brothers and sisters to keep the same silence you have asked of me. I don't need to meet and/or know your grandchildren if that is too embarrassing. They are not a priority for me.

You both struggled a lot to take care of, love, nurture and give to your children all that you were financially and emotionally capable of doing. I know, or at least can imagine, that this was often incredibly difficult and trying and was done at great sacrifice to you both. And I know there were difficulties with some of the children and that was heartbreaking and scary and emotionally draining They all, it appears, have turned out exceptionally well. This is due, I believe, more than anything else to the love and support they received from you. I now there was not an abundance of money but there was never a shortage of love.

I love and like you both very much and want us to continue to develop our relationship. It is painful for me though to maintain a level of respect because it feels as if you are not respecting me. I am to keep silent, to respect you and your needs while totally discounting mine. You gave everything you could to my brothers and sisters—all I ask is that you acknowledge that I exist.

This is a major request and one that I have struggled with but know that I cannot and will not wait forever or until you are both gone. I will proceed in any way that you wish but I will proceed. I know that feels like a threat but it is a statement about what I need and want and I will try to do it in any way that lessens your anxiety. You can tell them, individually and/or in any order that you want—or I can. You know them and probably have a sense of who might be the most accepting—and perhaps underestimate the ability of your own children to be accepting—and I am willing to test the waters with whoever you feel might be the best first one to know.

This does not have to be done before Christmas or anytime that soon, but I would hope for some time early in 1996 So please, take some time and think about this and hopefully we will be able to sit down and discuss this further. Last year you asked what I wanted for Christmas—the wish has not changed.

I love you.

The letter helped, and today, after having met the scores of siblings and nieces and nephews, and grand nieces and nephews I am still in awe. We hang a total of 65 Christmas stockings! I remember where every meeting took place and how amazing it was. There have been some incredible highs and a few truly difficult lows, but oh the highs are so worth all the difficulties as I became the clearly recognized and loved older/oldest sister. I feel so loved and blessed to have this wonderful finally storied family.

Judy Stone, Ph.D. served as a Peace Corps Volunteer in the early 60's in North Borneo (Sabah) and later worked for the Peace Corps in the selection and training of new volunteers to work in Thailand, Micronesia, Malaysia and Nepal. Upon completion of her MA in clinical psychology she returned to work overseas and then took a year off to fulfill her continued love of travel and adventures in Asia, Africa and Europe. Back home she began a 25-year relationship as a mental health consultant to the Job Corps, a program to train and educate high school drop-outs. It was during this time that she completed her doctorate at Loyola University and established a private practice in Chicago. Now retired, Judy is working on her soon to be released memoir, *A Stone's Throw,* from which this piece is excerpted.

Healing Through the Darkness

V. Falcón Vázquez

There's this deep consciousness inside me, a liberating voice that climbs out of my logic. My body is a vehicle for this soul, my mouth a tongue twister of truth and my voice can't stay silent.

~V. Falcón Vázquez

Here I am. Through the years, I've discovered different parts of who I am. We keep building and digging through ourselves. At least I know I have. I held on to the past for so long, but now I've discovered why. I needed to reconcile every part of my history. I needed to acknowledge every part of my pain. I had to open wounds to heal them better. We've heard that there's no instruction booklet on life, well, there's also no instruction booklet to healing. However, there is guidance when you ask for it. It will come in the simplest of forms. Be sure to open your heart to notice them. Guidance comes as a tickling in your gut, a deep resounding breath, a step towards the right direction, a flower where there was none, a bird soaring through the sky, a song, a word, an echo, a person, a picture, a call, a light, a star, a smile, and all the small and simple pleasant things we forget to see when we let worry, fear, hurt and shame overpower us.

I need you to understand one thing, if you are hurting, look inside. Begin the work of falling in love with the only person that knows you and loves you:

You.

I am healing:
This body is failing me again
This mind is playing games
This soul knows how it begins
How it should end.

I am healing,
Past, present and future
Struggles
Stories

Memories
Footprints.

I am
Interweaving connections,
Will we ever stop feeling?

One day, I prayed for healing, I prayed for all the pain to go away. I prayed to fill this void inside my heart. I prayed and prayed night and day. I asked *God, The Universe, PadreMadre, Gaia, Fuente de Luz, Fuente de Amor Universal, Fuente Divina de Todo Poder y Sanación*, to come and heal me. I called my ancestors, the warrior women, the healing mothers, the grandmothers, the leaders, the guides, I called and called and called them all. I had unconsciously woken up long ago. Until I finally heard, until I finally stopped and listened.

To heal, hurts.
Trying to understand
The unknown
Through reason
Through divinity
Nothing seems to work
My life lacks balance
But it's inevitable

When the pain is so real
No one understands
Even when they say they do
Because it's my story
It's my time
It's my learning
It's my divine intervention.

To heal, hurts.
To heal
is to know
Compassion
Love
Future
Self.

I laid for days, broken in the darkness, in the heaviness and pain of this body. I filled rivers with my tears, rivers that drowned me when I couldn't flow. There were days I hit my chest pretending my hands were a defibrillator and it would help stop my heart from hurting. I needed to begin again. I needed one more breath. I did not comprehend how one dies alive, how one grieves the loss of self, how one pulls apart to build back up. I took long showers with tears, I hugged my skin, I purged this containment of darkness, I trembled, and kneeled, feeling all of the lives before me crying. I had finally surrendered, accepted that vulnerability meant humility and compassion. I accepted the hurt that I carried for myself and for the world. I was afraid, afraid to collapse, to put my pride aside and say I was not ok. I had to learn that when the soul has had enough, it will knock you down and it will make you cry. I had always been good at swallowing my pain. I had been good at taking back the tears until my heart erupted with disaster.

SANAR

Carne,
fruto de la vida
te doy la sangre:
latir vibrante.
Riega el alma
con besos musicales,
que no te dé miedo ser
la tempestad en la calma
pero no olvides
curar el tiempo frágil
el árbol cortado antes de tiempo.
Niña viajera
que pisas el cielo rojo
mujer fértil

madre divina,
fortalece tu núcleo
la esencia de ti.

TO HEAL

Flesh,
Life's bounty
I give you my blood:
Vibrant throb.
Water thy soul
With musical kisses,
Be not afraid
To be the storm in the quietness
But don't forget
To heal the fragile time
The tree cut down before its time.
Wanderer
Who steps on the red sky
Fertile woman
Divine mother,
Strengthen your source
The essence of you.

Become confident dancing in your room, be free. Learn to love your own skin, your body is your temple, your vessel of love. I just want to let you know that you are okay. We learn to love through the loss and the chaos.

We learn to love even through our darkness, our self-struggle. We learn to love in between the fire and through the smoke. We learn to love in the middle of nowhere with no home. We learn to love with holes in our shoes. We learn to love with fear in our bones. We learn to love with broken dreams. We learn to love after all and all. And remember, just as we are, the earth is also a living soul. What we do to the earth, we do to ourselves. Let's take care of us too.

Be in harmony with yourself and everything that is surrounding you. Be in unity with who you are and all of who you are made to be. Be. Be. Be. Be in wholeness. Be mindful of your struggles and then we will find peace within thyself.

The world is turning red
The world is on fire
Fall is here
All is red
Yet, it's starting to cool down out there

Fall is here
We are burning
Turning into ashes
Learning how to die

How there's cycles
And there's amber tones of red

We are green
There is water in me
For the roots
Of my ancestry

There's yellow
Everything in the ground is yellow
The gold is hidden under the trees
Through the leaves
Like thunder it rolls to the sky

It brings joy
Like crispy afternoons
An evening of skies
A brilliant blue
Of unique tones you can never describe

Light, shadow, everything in between
All worlds combined
Never afraid
Never forgotten
Never broken
Never surrendered
Always knowing
Of the intellect and soul
We are never divided
Even if we try

To look for all the excuses
That "mankind"
Can invent

We shall all coexist
We are each other's
Valor
Compassion
Creation
New understandings
Forgiveness
Redemption
We are
The children
Of the universe
The love
Of all creation
The creation
Of Love.

Falcón Vázquez is a contemporary poet shedding light on so-cial, cultural and gender issues through the awareness of self. Integrating body, mind, and spirit she allows the audience to become aware of their own identities and realities shifting the perspective that even though we go through our own sto-ries we are not alone. In her work she has created a fusion of different writing styles giving a unique life to each poem chal-lenging the norms of poetry and many times prefers to write in free verse venturing out to experience an abstract truth. By creating space for magical realism, healing verses, and raw emotions Falcón Vázquez, has discovered poetry as a medi-cine for the heart and soul.

What My Daughter Knows

Marilyn Johnston

I stand shivering in the doorway
of a freezing cold room after a 30-hour
flight, my suitcase still in hand.
There's a No Trespass sign on the porch.
She came to Australia in winter,
to live in this—a condemned building!
She's a cook in some little Italian
restaurant just to scrape by,
earn a few bucks to keep her going
a few more months in this
land Down Under.

Another chapter in her smorgasbord life,
including: that pizza place on Liberty Street
in Salem, where she threw dough high
in the air, caught it expertly on her fists;
the deli on Burnside in Portland,
where she baked hard-crusted bread

and had to wash off white, flour-covered
dust from her hair each night;
the Lebanese place on Pine and Third
in Seattle, where she ladled out
huge platters of falafel and hummus,
found the secrets of baking baklava
so moist, I can still taste the honey
and rosewater-soaked filo on my tongue.

Later, she landed in Israel during
a Hezbollah raid and we were afraid.
But the letters she wrote
described how she'd learned six ways
to make brisket; gave us the recipe
for hamentashen she'd served
after stuffing the pastry with dates
she'd picked from the tree by her bunk.
Six months later, when she arrived home,
we sat cross-legged on the floor
of a Moroccan restaurant
and, afterwards, I had technicolor dreams till
    dawn—
whirling, whirling, scarves billowing,
spinning dervish of light—a sumptuous table
of fruits and nuts stretched before us.

I think of that now as I sit
in the hot bath water she's boiled for me
in this frozen building in Melbourne.
I lie back. My eyes are closed.
Suddenly, I hear the sounds of pans
clanging on the hot plate, her make-shift
stove, in the corner of the room.
Then, delicious smells. Some exotic
stew she's created for me,
permeates the air.
And it finally dawns on me,
what my daughter knows—
this business of starting
from nothing. Making it work.
Making it hers.

I Went to Bed with an Unfinished Poem in My Mouth

© 2021 Marilyn Johnston

Count the days since you walked further
than the fence line. Pull open the sliding
window. Recall all the times you've made
it through alive. Scroll the words
no darlo por sentado (don't take it for
    granted)
with your finger, on the cold surface of the
    glass.

Listen for the sounds the night makes.
Pretend the deer hunkering down beneath
the oak tree gives you advice about kindness.
Write what pains you, then throw it away.
Practice what you will say in gratitude—
in the morning, after the long silence,
when the protracted wait is over. Look up
at the *pink moon* as it rises. Dream as you
hear the cry of the wolf in the back field,
as you hold the poem in the palm of your
    hands—
howling for the breath to soak your face in.

Marilyn Johnston is an Oregon writer and filmmaker. She received an Oregon Literary Fellowship for Writers and is the author of two poetry collections, RED DUST RISING (2004), about her family's recovery from war, which was nominated for the Pushcart Prize; and BEFORE IGNITING (published in February 2020). She is the winner of the Donna J. Stone National Literary Award for Poetry and a Robert Penn Warren Award. Marilyn serves as a writing instructor in the Artists-in-the-Schools program, primarily working with at-risk and incarcerated youth.

"What Mahler Tells Me"

2021 John C Fraraccio

John C. Fraraccio

As I prepare for retirement from a profession that is utterly bereft of any sense of humor and prepare to spend more time in a world that seems increasingly bereft of same, I need reorganize and reallocate my time and other resources to keep the day and the waking part of the night from flowing unimpeded into the next installment. Reading so many words will play a large part in my scattered plans, possibly writing them as well, but so will music that has no words at all—or does it?

I am neither musician nor musicologist, and likely the only person you know who burned himself replacing the batteries in a portable radio. As for my choice of music I can only quote Duke Ellington twice: *There are only two kinds of music, good music and the other kind*, and *If it sounds good, it's good.*

I lean toward classical music in all its flavors. I thank my parents for the inclination, for each was a musician if only to the extent that each knew how difficult it was to become and remain one. They knew what they liked and returned to it throughout their lives. I got to learn what I liked, and still like.

I can savor all the flavors and appreciate the virtuosity displayed while both hearing and seeing a live or recorded performance and concert. That too takes practice. One insight is how an entire section of an orchestra can sound like one instrument, "the strings" in particular.

I am especially fond of the "tone poem" that is designed to evoke imagery of a select and specified theme. I try to guess at that imagery with each listen without first "reading the program."

And then there is Gustav Mahler, a late-Romantic composer who loudly disclaimed "program music" at least for his symphonic works but was not shy with lyrics. When words are not involved, he still tries to tell me something, and of all the classical composers whose works I have listened to he tries the hardest yet makes it all look (or sound) easy.

I leave his biography to his biographers. He was a troubled yet deeply philosophical man with a "Type A" personality, and an in-demand professional conductor (including the New York Philharmonic) and arranger of other composers' music. He wrote songs, principally setting poetry to music, and usually accompanied by an orchestra. (My German helps me "find my way around the kitchen" but I can deal with the end product.) He also was not shy about borrowing from his own works in composing his later works.

But he wrote no operas or operettas, no chamber music that he at least completed, or any concertos or sonatas that showcased one musical instrument. Instead, Mahler wrote large and for everyone involved, at times for larger-than-average orchestras and choruses (in one case much larger). I am convinced that the larger the scale and scope of his work the more intimate the thoughts and sentiments he tried to convey through his work. Some of his works were later "reduced" by others for smaller chamber or ensemble orchestras.

With one exception I focus on his symphonies and the impressions each provides this listener. You will hear at least one, or part of one, of the following in each of them: A dance, a march, and something that will give you pause. Parts of some symphonies sound cinematic, which is of note for a composer who passed away in 1911. There is not one wasted or superfluous note in any of them. Mahler was specific as to how he wanted them played but left their interpretation to others. As a conductor he knew what an orchestra could do, and as a composer I do not doubt he knew what an orchestra should not do.

If any of this is your introduction to Mahler, do not try it all at once or even by numbers but do strive to listen to each without interruption. And first confine your listen to headphones or speakers, then find and view a concert performance. Of the latter I purposely do not identify a choice but do note there is none I would not recommend. To me at least that is a signal of what Mahler requires.

So, what does Mahler tell me in so many notes if not words?

His First Symphony, "Titan," was first published after several performances and ensuing revisions. Each movement is a painting, and the first needs no clue from me as to its imagery. The third movement was my effective introduction to him, and if you do not recognize its theme then ask a friend who does. Rare is a symphony from which its composer removes a movement, but "Blumine" surfaces in the occasional performance.

His Second, "Resurrection," pretty much starts the same way, with its first two movements nearly ending the same way. With the fourth movement the mood noticeably changes, a singer enters the stage, and by the final movement a lot more enters the mix along with a cathedral organ. When it concludes you will conclude that you have heard something very special.

Be well rested for his Third, the longest and with an opening movement that runs as long as some others' entire symphonies. Each of its six movements bears a title that indicates Mahler himself sought and listened for inspiration. Hang your hat on those titles if you like, but let this one carry you along to its very end.

His Fourth is about childhood, possibly a lost one. I had planned the first and third movements as intermezzos to a stage performance of "The Diary of Anne Frank." I cannot explain why; they simply fit. The final movement is a hymn, of sorts.

His Fifth is his PTSD symphony. A soldier returns from war, is encouraged to rejoin Life, finds that he cannot, at least not entirely, but also finds triumph in simply managing. You very likely have heard its fourth movement as background music. To me that "song without words" is not so much about love lost but unconsummated.

His Sixth is about a life well-lived and with enough time to reflect, then foreseeably yet quite suddenly ended. You hear muted cowbells, a very large hammer strike twice, and a finale that I guarantee will startle you.

His Seventh bears a title that was not his idea but provides enough of a clue at least to me that it is all a dream, or series of dreams, that made the dreamer thankful for having awakened, or for that matter having slept. It is his most muscular work and by no means soporific. Cowbells ring too, and you do indeed hear a mandolin.

If his Eighth is not his longest it is certainly his largest. This choral symphony is not the "Symphony of a Thousand" for nothing, and though it is in two discrete parts there are distinct movements that bring everyone you can possibly think of into the sonic picture. In sum it is about creation if not Creation and triumphantly so. If you like to read lyrics in translation then this is the set to start with, then return to his Second, Third and Fourth; you will notice a connection.

Mahler knew how to say goodbye. The first and final movements of his Ninth are heartbreaking, and the final ten or so minutes in concert have a unique impact on an audience that customarily focuses on the conductor. Compare that with "The Farewell" from his "Song of the Earth" cycle with orchestra that I have heard sung by a baritone, a contralto, and a mezzo-soprano; in short, with gravity.

He wrote only part of his Tenth while others made the available fragments into a "performable" whole after his death. Some conductors will not touch it simply because they feel Mahler did not compose it in its entirety. An intact slow movement touches on what his Ninth does but perhaps not quite as cheerfully. Judge this symphony on its own merits instead of as a Mahler-wannabe.

So, what does Mahler still tell me? Life is complicated and short and worth every minute it takes to keep your eyes, mind and heart open. No matter what troubles come your way, whether or not you are the cause, you live. And even when you die, you live.

Now listen to the final movement of his Third, again if appropriate, from start to finish. Its final, prolonged note is nothing less than the Word.

—Feast of Saint James the Apostle, 2020

John C. Fraraccio, New Jerseyan who knows Oregon well thanks to friends, student, library aide and volunteer, short order cook and server, shoe salesman, mail carrier, typesetter, beat reporter, news and copy editor, print production specialist, actor and stage director, lawyer, student.

Living in a Balanced World

Carolyn Clarke

How many times have you heard the phrase, 'There is safety in numbers'? Parents constantly tell their children to not walk home from school alone, don't walk on the street alone, and don't go to the mall alone because being in a group provides not only companionship, but discourages the approach of strangers with unknown intentions.

While some animals are loners, many others live in groups for the same reason. Lions, wolves, elephants, and zebra, to name a few, prefer a social life which offers many advantages—more eyes watching for predators, more individuals to fight off predators, thus the increased ability to protect the young, old, or injured, and in the case of omnivores, more individuals to ensure successful hunting. And yes, to provide companionship and someone to snuggle with when it gets cold. An ominous sight indeed is a ring of bison, with the most vulnerable in the center, facing off against formidable adversaries, sharp horns and hooves at the ready. Whatever predator was thinking about a calf snack would be wise to reconsider. Schools of fish and flocks of birds, sometimes with hundreds or even thousands of members, can turn on a dime to confuse and make it much harder for an approaching predator to single out just one individual.

Being in a group also spreads out the workload. One of my favorite sights (and sounds) is a flock of geese flying in their familiar V formation honking all the way. They take turns leading the flock so the lead goose doesn't get too tired. The reason for the V is so that each bird can draft off the one in front of them reducing wind resistance thus saving energy. Geese can fly 70% longer this way before they need to stop for a rest than if each goose flew by itself.

Family groups of the same species cooperating is a common sight, but what about animals of different species deciding to join forces? We've all seen the cute videos of unlikely friendships between dogs and cats, cows and dogs, horses and cats, a dog and a duck. All kinds of combinations between domestic animals and even domestic and wild animal friendships: the dog and a deer, a cat and a dolphin, a tortoise and a hippo (actually that one was in a zoo, but pretty cool nevertheless), and a pretty amazing video of a husky playing with a polar bear. Combinations of animals that could have had a very unhappy outcome, but didn't. Unusual combinations of animals that became BFFs.

The natural world is sometimes seen as cruel and harsh, and many times it is, but, as with many things, there are always exceptions to the rule. Nature can also be resilient, surprising and even creative. Mutualism, as defined by Merriam Webster, is a "mutually beneficial association between different kinds of organisms". In other words, an arrangement that's a win-win for both individuals.

Animals with different skill sets are more successful at finding dinner and sharing it. Coyotes and badgers are often seen hunting together—the coyote can run faster to capture prey, but if the prey goes to ground in a burrow, the badger's excellent digging skills can still win the day. Ravens and wolves are known allies. An eye in the sky can often find vulnerable prey or recent kills more readily than a nose to the ground. In return the wolves' sharp teeth and strong jaws can more easily tear open a carcass giving ravens access to the meat inside and a share of the spoils. A more unusual pairing occurs in the ocean. Groupers, particularly in the Red Sea, are sometimes seen with a hunting buddy. In fact, they have been seen with a couple different species, both moray eels or octopus in tow. The grouper is a good hunter alone, but if the prey hides among the corals, a slim moray eel or a long octopus tentacle can fit where the grouper can't go.

The most interesting of all is when predator and prey call a truce, wave a white flag and declare an area a 'no kill' zone. One example is the wrasse, that sets up a 'cleaning station'. In this case the wrasse clean their 'clients' of parasites, even entering their gills and mouth to do so and trust that even much larger fish that would normally consider them a lovely hors d'oeuvre, won't take advantage of their vulnerable situation.

Did you know that some female tarantulas have pet frogs? Well, maybe 'pet' is exaggerating slightly. Perhaps nursemaid would be a more apt description. Some tarantulas

eat frogs and toads, but the Columbian less-
erblack tarantula takes exception to the dot-
ted humming frog. Scientists say the
tarantula distinguishes this particular frog by
smell and offers it a home in its burrow and
even protects it from other predators. In return the frog eats ants and other smaller insects that could harm the spider's eggs thus
upping the chances of their survival.

The Nile crocodile can grow more than
16 feet in length and weigh over 1,600
pounds. It eats fish, mammals, other reptiles
and birds. However, there is one bird that has
become an ally—the Egyptian plover, also fit-
tingly called the crocodile bird. True, it's a
small bird and probably wouldn't make much
of a meal, but its relationship with the crocodile is still pretty audacious. The crocodile is
a voracious eater, but like the rest of us occa-
sionally gets food stuck between its teeth. And
since Dental floss isn't readily available, it's
the plover's job to pick the food out between
the crocodile's teeth. The plover gets a free
meal and the crocodile doesn't get infections.

My question is how did all of these relationships start? How did all of these coali-
tions become a 'thing'? Who was the first
grouper who thought, "I wonder if Fred, two

corals down, could help get me something to eat." Or maybe it was the moray eel who started the whole thing by watching the grouper hunting. I can imagine that the relationship between the frog and tarantula may have started by accident—a case of the frog finding itself at the wrong place at the wrong time. But who was the first tarantula to understand that having a frog around helped ensure the survival of her eggs? Did some of the youngster spiders when they got older think, "Remember that pet frog we had as kids? I want one of those." And what hungry plover saw a perhaps weakened crocodile and wandered close enough to think, "My what sharp teeth you have. Oh look, food. Can I get that for you?" And who was the first crocodile to determine it was in its own best interest NOT to eat that plover?

No matter how these relationships began, these are just a few examples of some pretty inspiring partnerships. Many animals are capable of observational learning. In each instance, perhaps it took just one hungry, brave, intrepid, out-of-the-box, forward-thinking critter to start a trend. Or maybe it was just an excellent debater. There may be a few cases of, "You ate my Uncle Frank. Find somebody else to pick the food out of your teeth." But in the end, cooperation won.

A balanced ecosystem means each organism playing their role in a diversified world. The maned wolf is a South American cousin to the gray wolf. It is an omnivore, but half of its diet is fruit and vegetables. It has a particular relationship with lobeira, a plant also known as 'wolf apple' for reasons that will become clear in a moment. The plant itself is a flowering shrub that bears fruit that is almost 50 percent of the maned wolf's diet and contains several hundred seeds. similar to a tomato. When the wolf defecates, which is often on nests of leaf cutter ants, the seeds are dispersed. The ants have fungus gardens which they fertilize with the wolf dung. The wolf apple seeds are later discarded, but the entire process helps germinate the seeds. The natural world is inextricably linked. Eliminating one animal, insect, or plant is when things go awry. That's when the cycle is broken.

If animals can figure these things out, as the supposedly more intelligent being, humans should be able to as well. We are all the same species, but if we can learn anything from the rest of the natural world, we don't have to look alike or think alike in order to be

BFFs. It's in our best interest to have each other's backs. We accomplish more together. We become a balanced system when no one is left behind. We are all connected. Each of us has a role to play. Each of us belongs.

Carolyn Clarke has a passion for the natural world and all critters great and small. She has a degree in Psychology with an emphasis in Animal Behavior from Smith College's Ada Comstock program. She has lived in Iowa, New York, Colorado, Massachusetts and spent three years in Georgia caring for some very special great apes. Carolyn currently is retired and living in Rhode Island.

Nobody Knows You

Jean Sheldon

Susan had little doubt, as she snapped the final clasp on her guitar case, that the uninspired set she'd just finished would be her last. Her exhaustion as she slid into her coat far exceeded the energy expended in a few hours of performing. All she wanted at that moment was to collect her pay and go home. Her eyes adjusted to the dark side of the stage lights and scanned the dimly lit club for its owner, finally spotting him at the bar. It wasn't surprising to find Mario wrapped around an animated blond in an abbreviated dress sporting an overzealous application of makeup.

"Hey, Mario. I'm finished. You owe me a hundred and twenty bucks."

He detached from the blond and spun the bar stool to face her. "I don't know if I should pay you for that last set. You stunk."

"Yeah, I get that way when I'm dodging beer bottles."

"It was only one, and you could have ignored the jerk. He wouldn't have thrown it if you hadn't flipped him off."

A response seemed pointless. "Can you pay me?"

While Mario grudgingly took money from the cash register, Susan studied the crowd. In the few years since she began playing there, jeans and tennis shoes gave way to stiletto heels and sequins dresses. Musical preferences had changed too. Not just in Mario's club, but around Chicago. Acoustic instruments and unamplified voices required a quiet audience and faced fierce competition from high powered, high volume bands and DJs.

The rest of her group had seen the future and made the transition to more profitable genres than their more traditional music. Susan could listen to a variety of styles, but she preferred the less formulated, raw emotion of folk and acoustic blues when she played. She had declined their invitation to join them, which might have been professional suicide, but giving up the music she loved seemed a suicide of the soul. Had she blown it? At forty, going back to school or starting a new career seemed unlikely. She wanted to play her music, but if bars and clubs no longer wanted acoustic bands, earning a living could be a problem.

"Here." Mario handed her six twenties that likely contained enough illegal substances to get her arrested. "I'll call when I need ya'."

She shoved the bills in her pocket and withheld comment until the outer front door closed behind her. "I won't hold my breath."

The temperature had dropped twenty degrees since her arrival four hours earlier, and an inch of snow coated every surface. That pleased her city weary heart. The glistening blanket muffled a layer of noise and transformed the normally depressing neighborhood into a sparkling wonderland. She glanced over her shoulder and chuckled at the solitary trail of footprints that marked her passage. If she'd had the energy to extract her phone and snap a picture, she'd have called it "Portrait of a musician out of step with the times." Amused, but distracted by the gloomy thought, she hadn't noticed a snow-covered plastic wrapper. When her foot made contact, it slid, which threw her off balance and sent her crashing to the sidewalk.

"Ouch."

Susan remained where she had fallen for a moment to collect her thoughts and test various body parts. She tilted her head from side to side and rotated her shoulders, then flexed both arms and both legs with a sense of relief. Nothing seemed damaged, and a quick glance around offered the additional consolation that no one had seen her fall. Using the guitar case for support, she made it from her knees to a standing position, and was brushing off accumulated snow and humiliation as the bus arrived.

The big box Guild guitar she played weighed almost twenty pounds in its hardshell case and required effort to maneuver through the narrow doors and up steep stairs to board the bus. She was comforted that at the end of her trek she found a driver who, obviously accustomed to navigating city traffic, had a Zen-like calm and a smile. Susan returned the smile, waved her transit card over the farebox and obeyed the silent green light that urged her along.

The bus was empty except for one other passenger. A large black woman sat on the first side seat behind the driver. She looked up as Susan approached. "Ah, a musician. You any good or do you just carry that thing around for show?" A wrist full of bracelets jangled as she gestured at the guitar.

Susan took the bench opposite her traveling companion and slid the guitar behind her legs. The woman had knitting needles in her hands and a colorful piece of fabric in her lap. "I'm good." She answered without thinking and was slightly embarrassed by how conceited her remark must have sounded. "I mean, I do okay, but musical tastes seem to be changing. The band they hired for the second half of the night had more volume and a bigger following."

"Oh, I hear you, honey. What kind of music do you play?"

"Blues and folk mostly. I play some contemporary stuff to get work."

"I'm a blues singer, myself. My name's Rosie, and I came to Chicago from the Delta in 1945, right after the end of the Second World War. Back then, you could walk up and down Maxwell Street and sit in with musicians from all over the country, hell, all over the world, and 'til all hours of the morning."

Susan thought the woman had confused her dates. She couldn't have been more than 60. "Glad to meet you Rosie, I'm Susan."

"So, tell me, girl, why are you so mournful?"

Surprised by the comment, and more than a little miffed that Rosie guessed how rotten she felt, Susan shook her head as she replied. "I'm not much of an actress either, am I? The clubs around town are changing. I knew it would happen eventually, but most of the places are switching to rock bands and putting in DJs and dance floors. Acoustic music isn't much in demand."

"So, you're givin' up?" The knitting fell to her lap and a half smile suggested there was more to the comment then its brevity implied. Susan sensed it was a challenge and the knitter's next sentence confirmed it. "Bring that axe out of its cozy little sleeping compartment and let's see if you got anything worth saving."

After her less than stellar performance at the bar, Susan was eager to prove herself and unpacked the guitar with more energy than she'd felt all evening. As she adjusted the strap and checked the tuning, she glanced at the driver who gave a smile and a nod of approval. It was only then that she noticed the quiet that permeated her surroundings. She could see they were moving, yet the engine noise was negligible. There was no creaking metal, no whoosh of air-brakes, and no outside traffic noises penetrating the thin walls and multiple windows. That level of silence in the muted fluorescent lights gave the scene a mystical quality.

Rosie had returned to her knitting and was humming a song Susan knew well, *Nobody Knows You When You're Down and Out*. The tune was written by blues musician Jim Cox in 1923, but it was made popular by one of her favorite singers, Bessie Smith. Without taking her eyes off Rosie, Susan squeezed the bronze strings against the rosewood neck and followed along as she sang.

Nobody knows you when you're
down and out
In your pocket, not one penny
And your friends, you haven't any
And as soon as you get on your feet
again
Everybody is your long-lost friend

It's mighty strange, without a doubt,
but
Nobody wants you when you're
down and out

With a grateful nod to decades of calluses on her fingertips, Susan pushed, pulled, strummed, plucked and pinched the yielding strings. Her efforts produced more than mere background for Rosie's powerful voice; they filled barely perceptible spaces in the quivering air with a passion Susan knew had been missing from her music for some time. When the singer paused for a breath, the guitarist filled the gap with a soul soothing 12 bar blues riff that she had never played better. And when Rosie rejoined, Susan and the bus driver added vocal harmonies.

"Nobody knows you," Rosie wailed the last stanza, stretching octaves like rubber bands. "Nobody knows you." Her voice, deep and throaty, resounded the length and breadth of their private arena. "I said, nobody knows you when you're down and out."

With the final note still echoing, Rosie roared with laughter and tipped her chin at Susan. "You're pretty good, girl. You got a fine voice and you coax sweetness from that guitar the way a mama coaxes smiles from her baby." Sparkles, like flickering stars in a summer sky, danced across Rosie's obsidian eyes. "So, I'll ask you again, do you plan on givin' up? Gettin' into another kind of work, like night shifts at a convenience store. That ought to give you good reason to sing the blues." She leaned back in the seat, nodding gently. "You know, child, we all have something to give in this life. We're here to do that. Share what we got. Don't miss your chance to do what you came to do."

Before Susan had digested the comment, the driver yelled "Hang on." There was a loud noise and Susan thought the bus had slammed into something. She tried to grab the nearby support bar, but missed and her head flew back into the window.

"Hey, are you all right?" Susan heard a voice and realized she was lying on a sidewalk that was covered in snow. "Can you hear me?" The question came from a man in his midtwenties who knelt at her side.

"What happened? Where's the bus?"

"What bus?"

"The bus I was on. I think it hit something and I slammed my head against the window." She looked frantically at her guitar case. "Where's my guitar?"

Frowning at Susan and the large object that lay beside her, he pulled out a cell phone. "That looks like a guitar to me, Lady. Maybe I'd better call an ambulance. I saw you fall when I came out of Mario's. When you didn't get right up, I came running. Did you hit your head on the sidewalk?"

"No. I hit it on the window." She touched a tender spot on the back of her head. "How long have I been laying here?"

"Only a few seconds. Your eyes were open when I got to you. Do you want me to call?" He held the phone in her face.

"No. Thanks. I'm okay." Her voice trembled slightly as she climbed to her knees. When her rescuer saw her struggle, he stood and grabbed her elbow to assist. "I think I might wave down a cab, though. I'm not ready for another bus ride."

Susan closed the apartment door and leaned her guitar against the wall, hastily opening the laptop. She had spent the cab ride considering events of the evening, and none of it made sense. Rosie's style was familiar, but it wasn't any contemporary blues singer. The whole thing had to have been a dream or some strange kind of altered consciousness from the bump on her head. How could so much have happened in the few seconds she lay on the sidewalk?

The woman had said her name was Rosie and that she came to Chicago from the Delta after World War II. Susan entered the words "Delta" "Rosie" and "blues" in the search engine and followed the first link to a blues women's website. Leaning forward for a closer look, she was shocked to recognize the face of the woman on the bus in a photo. According to the article, she was known as Delta Rose, and behind her, with his hands on her shoulders, stood her son, Charles, the bus driver. The story went on to say that Delta Rose had died in 1963 and Charles in 1987. There was another photograph supposedly taken a month before her passing. Under it was a quote from the singer: "I'm gonna spend the rest of my days and then some, keeping the blues alive."

"Wow, Rosie, you weren't kidding." Susan smiled as she closed the laptop and retrieved her guitar, remembering the mix of embarrassment and pleasure she felt at Rosie's words. They gave her a new confidence and sense of purpose, and left no doubt about what life had intended her to share. No matter what the future might bring, she intended to share it. "Okay," she said to her guitar. "Let's see if we can coax a little sweetness out of you, for Rosie, for Charles and so I don't miss the chance to do what I came to do."

Jean Sheldon is a dabbler in fine and graphic arts, music, poetry and mystery writing. To pay the rent, she has tended bar, driven a cab, landscaped, worked as a switchboard operator, a respiratory therapist, an assistant to a nuclear chemist and performed a myriad of tasks in service jobs. Born and raised in Chicago, she has relished life in many parts of Illinois, Wisconsin, Colorado, New Mexico and currently, Oregon. She credits the constant motion and changing scenery with exposing the great beauty of this country and its people, and revealing the truth that we are more alike than we know. www.jeansheldon.com

The Gift

Rosalyn Kliot

This poem is a celebration of life written at the beginning of COVID-19 when I inhaled spring...and I include a few observations...and a few suggestions on muddling through.

Spring is breathing itself into existence,
With each puff, a tiny bud,
A golden hue,
A touch of pink,
A shimmer of blue.
Silent words of joy and peace.

Streaming sun awakening earth,
Love's glory, enfolding all.
We glow in warmth and comfort pure,
The safe and sane rebirth of life.
We breathe it in,
We hear the call.

Pandemic Musings

© 2021 Rosalyn Kliot

I admit to being an optimist but also a realist. This is a golden opportunity to discover yourself, to go inward, and find the great companion and friend to yourself... you.

Re-discover your childhood passions... they are still within you. If you don't play music or do art, then listen to music and look at art. These simple acts have almost the same positive effects on the brain.

Exercise, meditate, read, connect with friends and family in healthful ways, eat well...and take good care of your mental state. Stress and anxiety lower resistance, and impact the immune system. Nothing lasts forever... keeping a joyful attitude will get us through this crazy time somewhat less scathed. We are resilient. Attitude is everything.
Use this time to forgive everyone everything... forgiveness does not excuse... it frees the soul...

let go of resentment, anger, hatred, and fear... think of today
as the last day of your life... How will it be spent?

Focus on what you love... just love.

Healing Trauma

© 2021 Rosalyn Kliot

Dive into it... without fear... feel it...

Breathe it... and then... watch it...

As the observer... it is chrysalis... dissolving

Crystals... see it shimmer...

Embrace it... it is nothing

No thing...

Rosalyn Kliot is an award winning and published artist, a speaker, and an occasional writer. Her art and essays have been published in various and diverse publications, books, and journals. She has self-published a number of books, one of which has been digitized and is archived at the United States Holocaust Museum in D.C. She is a retired certified Vocational Rehabilitation Counselor and Forensic Expert Vocational Witness at Federal hearings. Currently, she fills her days with studio time, and hiking the scenic trails of the Pacific Northwest.

Writing to Wes

Lori L. Lake

With the pandemic and wildfires and protests (oh, my!), sometimes it's been difficult to maintain a positive attitude. Reading for escape. Check. Listening to music that makes me feel. Check. Writing novels and staying creative. Half-check. Using videoconferencing to stay in touch with friends and loved ones during quarantine. Check. Am I doing all I can to be hopeful and healthy? Sometimes it hasn't felt like it.

At times, I haven't been able to resist viewing the news. It's been hard to keep myself from "doom-scrolling" on my phone. Hearing the frantic voices and screaming pundits only makes me feel helpless and hopeless though ... but it's also somehow strangely addictive.

I have been out of sorts and anxious for most of this current year. I have been alone in quarantine. I have embraced silences and felt lonely at times.

And then one day I ran across an article from The Marshall Project, the Emmy-nominated, nonprofit, online journalism organization focusing on issues related to criminal justice in the United States. They regularly feature pieces written by inmates, and on this day, I read an essay entitled, "The Cruel Irony of Social Distancing When You're in Solitary" by someone named Wesley Williams. The day I read it, I was on Day 75 of not having had a hug from anyone because of the 2020 Coronavirus pandemic. The writer's humorous attitude along with his astute observations caused me to think about human connection, about being loved and how much that's wrapped up in being able to touch people, to be close, to hug and be held, especially in times of stress and worry.

At the completion of the piece, a biographical note informed readers that the writer is incarcerated in New York where he is serving a maximum of 25 years for manslaughter and that he is a poet and a student at the Bard College Initiative.

How coincidental!

Just a few days earlier I happened to watch a four-part PBS documentary, "College Behind Bars," which the producers describe as an "inspiring, emotional, deeply human story of men and women struggling to earn college degrees while in prison for serious crimes. In four years of study they become scholars, shatter stereotypes, reckon with their pasts, and prepare to return to society. The film was truly a groundbreaking exploration of incarceration, injustice, race in America, and the transformative power of education."

So Bard College was the higher education facility that the documentary focused on and also the college with which Mr. Wilson was studying. Weird coincidence? Or something different?

I was so impressed with the article and its lighthearted humor. ("You may go crazy in here, but at least you won't get corona.") The writer was clear and concise, the descriptions were lively, his sentiments written with elegance. I reflected about that essay for several days. Here I'd been complaining because I was seven weeks into quarantining without physical human contact, and Mr. Williams had been stuck like that for a decade and a half. Big deal that I was on Day 75 Without a Hug; he was at *Year* 15+ Without a Hug.

My own brief period of separation from society was a mere drop in the bucket in comparison to his. Suddenly I felt blessed by my good fortune—so much so that I decided to write a thank you note to Mr. Williams. I told him that until the pandemic lockdown, I never fully realized how much I depend upon hugs, pats, shaking hands, casual arm punches, and just generally jostling with people I care about. I explained how I wasn't sure why I felt compelled to write to him, but I'd read the article on my phone's Newsfeed and found it to be thoughtful and well-written. I felt a calling to contact him as I kept puzzling about what it would be like to live one's life for *years and years* without much (or any) positive physical contact. I told him 75 days had been bad enough for me and I could hardly imagine how rough the years have been for him. I urged him to keep writing because he had Voice with a capital V.

A couple weeks later, a letter arrived with prison data printed on the envelope. Enclosed I found a handwritten letter thanking me for writing and telling me a little about him and his circumstances. He entered the criminal justice system at the age of 17 and has spent his entire adult life locked up. He was functionally illiterate when he arrived there. Back then, he was angry and lost and alone. Now he was grateful and thankful to connect with others—even without touch—because he welcomed that level of humanity.

At one point in one of my early letters to him, I asked if he, a 34-year-old incarcerated East coast Black man felt okay about corresponding with a 60-year-old West coast white lesbian. He said, "People should love one another. That's all. We should care about others because we are all in this together."

In the months that followed, I learned a great deal about Wes, and I shared a lot about myself. I came to understand that despite the surface differences, we have ever so much in common: rough childhoods, ineffective parental figures, living through injustices in this world, and dealing with hopelessness, anxiety, and, at times, depression. We are both fascinated by books, nuts about almost any kind of music, love our brothers and sisters desperately, and we share a liking for philosophers like Paulo Coelho and poets like Mary Oliver. I could probably write to Wes for the rest of my life, and I'd still learn new things about him—and new things about myself as well.

I have always believed that Black Lives Matter, but as a white person, every day is a new journey of learning more about the extent to which non-white people have suffered and are still suffering. Now that I'm nearing retirement age and have had health issues off and on for several years, I can't get out on the streets to march in downtown Portland or hold candlelight vigils before armed riot police or engage in many of the other tasks that need to be done to help attain equity and equal rights for Black, Indigenous, and People of Color. In my circumstances, contributing to the Movement—other than monetarily—is not so easy.

What I CAN do is write and talk to this one solitary person, a man young enough to be my son, and urge him not to give up hope and not to stop healing. One day, he'll be released from prison, and he'll need a lot of support to face a whole new world, one he left at the tender age of 17 and hasn't been back to ever since. He'll be preparing for a completely different set of experiences upon exit, and he must maintain a strong imagination and foster his own resilience in order to succeed.

My writer friend Sue Hardesty once told me a story about a man walking along the beach who noticed a boy picking up sea stars and gently throwing them into the ocean. The man asked him what he was doing, and the boy told him he was throwing starfish back into the water because the tide was going out, and if they got trapped on the beach, they would die. The man said, "Are you nuts? There's miles of beach and a kazillion of these critters. You can't make a difference." The boy picked up another sea star. He threw it into the ocean and grinned. He said:

"I'm pretty sure I made a difference for that one."

When Sue told that story a few years ago, I thought it was right on, and I've thought about it often over the years. Today it reminds me of an old adage from grade school: "Each one, teach one." What if we thought in terms of making a difference in one life rather than being paralyzed by the specter of all those people for whom help is needed?

What if every person endeavored to become acquainted with someone different from themselves—different in race or politics or religion or age or socio-economic level or felony status or gender or intelligence or whatever? What if we used our skills and gifts to reach out to someone who seemed less fortunate in some way—not giving money to a church fund or buying a goat for someone in Guatemala, which is pretty easy, but actually having regular contact with someone different, without passing any judgments or having expectations?

I believe we might discover how much we have in common with people who seem entirely different from ourselves.

Discovery is a wonderful thing. Curiosity is one of the most important qualities that human beings have always had. Education and life learning are critical to survival in this changing world. Why not give hope and help to someone else in order to satisfy their need (and your own!) for discovery and curiosity and learning? Doesn't everyone deserve hope and healing?

The great poet, memoirist, actress, and civil rights activist, Maya Angelou, once said, "If you learn, teach. If you get, give." As far as I can tell, isn't that pretty much the Golden Rule? "Do unto others as you would have them do unto you" is what St. Matthew wrote in the Gospel. (Unless you're a devoted masochist, in which case, please don't focus on this maxim.)

Learn, teach, get, give ... isn't that a great deal of what matters in life? It's not whoever dies with the most toys wins; it should be whoever dies with the most *love* wins.

I feel love and affection for Wesley Williams, yet I have never met him in person, and I may not meet him for years, if ever. But through the power of paper and pen—and an occasional phone call—two disparate people have touched one another's souls. He could have been my son or a neighbor or a young person I taught. Our lives didn't intersect that way, however. We "met" due to the power of a frank and honest essay.

Writing to Wes may turn out to help me more than it does him. Who can know? But I haven't had a black guy friend since my senior year in high school, and I'm delighted every time I find a letter from him in my mailbox. We wish for good things for one another, and I can't imagine losing contact with him.

We are both without embraces, but sometimes, Wes's letters feel like a hug.

Lori L. Lake is the author of a dozen novels and two short story collections. She's edited four anthologies, including

Lesbians on the Loose with Jessie Chandler, which won a Golden Crown Literary "Goldie" Award. Her short work is featured in over a dozen anthologies including *The Silence of the Loons, Time's Rainbow,* and *Women of the Mean Streets.* Lori's known for sharing writing craft resources and is especially fond of teaching about crime fiction and about writing short stories. In her spare time, she runs a small publishing house called Launch Point Press. Lori lives on the edge of Portland, Oregon, at the Fortress of Solitude/Sanctuary of Solace. http://www.LoriLLake.com

Now We Know: Healing the World

Donna Reynolds

Do the best you can until you know better. Then when you know better, do better.

~Maya Angelou

Eight years ago I was gripped by information that was so wonderful yet so simple and so logical it changed my life. I couldn't understand why I hadn't heard about it before or why everyone didn't know about it—and why most *still* don't know! Although some of this information has been discovered relatively recently, much has been around for decades but purposely suppressed by those it would financially impact. This suppression needs to end. We need to absorb, embrace, and *share* this information, make informed choices, and then *act* on them so we can finally heal ourselves, the animals, and the world.

In 2010, my mother and a very good friend both passed away from heart disease. They ate a standard American diet that included meat, dairy, and eggs. The information they received from their families, their doctors, and society said this was an approved and healthy way of eating, yet their diets and medications could not and did not prevent their heart disease.

In 2012, I watched the documentary, *Forks Over Knives*. It presented well-researched and eye-opening information that eating a diet based on fruits, vegetables, nuts, grains, and legumes and *excluding* meat, dairy, and eggs was the healthiest way to eat for humans, as well as being kinder to the animals and the planet. The information revealed that eating a plant-based diet could also strengthen your immune system and help fight chronic diseases such as obesity, diabetes, and hypertension, and could even *reverse* heart disease. Unfortunately, I learned of this exciting information two years too late to share with my mother and my friend.

In 2020, COVID-19, one of the most widespread of the viruses humans have contracted from animals, has infected millions and killed hundreds of thousands and continues infecting and killing throughout the world. Most who have died of COVID-19 had a weakened immune system due to having one or more chronic diseases—diseases that can be treated by a plant-based diet. There have been more than 10,000 studies from peer-reviewed journals, numerous documentaries, and a growing number of plant-based doctors who all agree that we can reduce our risk of getting these chronic diseases by up to 80 percent—that's 80%!—just by eating certain foods, like plants, and avoiding others, like meat. We have crucial information that we know will save lives and we need to get it out there.

HEALING OURSELVES

The food you eat can be either the safest and most powerful form of medicine or the slowest form of poison.

~Ann Wigmore

DOCTORS AND COMMITTEES

It's natural to assume our doctors received a comprehensive education in medical school and that they keep up-to-date on the latest medical information. But this is only partly true as medical schools offer few, if any nutrition classes in their program. Most doctors don't know of the numerous benefits of eating a whole foods, plant-based diet. Also, it is usually much faster, easier, and more financially beneficial for doctors to prescribe drugs and continue renewing them for our ongoing diseases—sometimes despite dangerous side effects—rather than showing us that it's often possible to take care of these illnesses once and for all by eating plants, with no side effects but better health. Many doctors (mainly those who are not plant-based themselves) don't mention that a plant-based diet can be helpful as they simply don't believe their patients will try it.

The doctors, the hospitals, and the pharmaceutical industry aren't the only ones who would suffer financially from a healthy population that thrived on eating just plants. In 1977, Senator George McGovern chaired a committee on Nutrition and Human Needs but after they released the first US dietary guidelines, the meat, dairy, and egg producers were not pleased. This report stated that the diet of the American people had become rich in meat, saturated fat, cholesterol, and sugar, and that the harmful effects from these substances represented as great a threat to our health as smoking. It stated that too much fat, sugar, and salt was directly linked to heart disease, cancer, obesity, stroke, and other killer diseases. The powerful meat, dairy, and egg producers did not want this information to reach the public and succeeded in dissolving the McGovern Committee by having the Agriculture Committee take over. Yes, Agriculture—the ones who *produce* the meat, dairy, and eggs which the report said *cause* our chronic diseases, and, due in part to that report being suppressed, still *are* the causes, four decades later.

So why are meat, dairy, and eggs as great a threat to our health as smoking? What is it about our Standard American Diet (SAD) that makes it so deserving of its acronym?

MEAT

Fiber and Cholesterol—These two substances reflect the basic differences between a plant-based and a meat-based diet. Fiber can help maintain a healthy weight, reduce the risk of diabetes and heart disease, and of course, prevent constipation! Plants are loaded with fiber; meat has none. Cholesterol is made in the liver, and the liver makes all we need, but we get additional cholesterol from eating certain foods. Too much cholesterol can lead to blockages, heart disease, and stroke. Meat, dairy, and eggs have cholesterol; plants have none.

Protein—Yes, meat has plenty of it, but so do plants, since that's where herbivores like horses and cows get their protein. In fact, both 100 grams of beans and 100 grams of beef *each* provide 22 grams of protein—but the cost of beans is a whole lot less!

Cancer—In October 2015, the World Health Organization classified processed meat, including hot dogs, hamburgers, bacon, and sausage as a carcinogen, and red meat, including beef, pork, and lamb was classified as a *probable* carcinogen. Although this alarming cancer classification from this reputable organization was announced five years ago, we continue to ignore it and the government still serves these foods to our children in their school lunches.

Fish—We're told to eat fish to get the essential fatty acids for brain and heart health. But salmon can be up to 50 percent fat and only a third of that is good omega-3—the rest is saturated and unsaturated fat. Plus, fish has no fiber, but does have cholesterol, with bass having about the same as beef! Better to stick with plant foods rich in omega-3 such as walnuts, edamame, and chia seeds and that don't contain pollutants like methylmercury that can be found in some fish higher up in the food chain like tuna.

DAIRY

Baby Cow—Unless you're a baby cow, milk does *not* do a body good. Adult humans, like other mammals, don't need milk after we've been weaned—especially not from a different species! Full of hormones and saturated fat, cow's milk is designed to grow a 60-pound calf into a 600-pound steer. No wonder it's hard to keep the weight off when we're downing lots of cheese, yogurt, and ice cream!

Diseases—Besides obesity, dairy products contribute to conditions such as acne, asthma, diabetes, heart disease, and even Alzheimer's. Dairy has also been linked to an increase in the risk of prostate, breast, and ovarian cancers.

Unfair and Unwanted—Having the government feed schoolchildren dairy products (along with cancerous processed meat) is not only unhealthy, but unfair, as the majority of African Americans, American Indians, and Asian Americans are lactose intolerant. And remember, we're feeding this inflammatory liquid to our kids not because it's good for them, but because the powerful dairy, meat, and egg industries suppressed vital nutritional information for their own financial benefit. The good news is that dairy milk sales have dropped while plant milk sales continue to climb. Unfortunately, subsidized dairies continue to produce so much unwanted excess milk that the US government now has a still-growing 1.4 *billion-pound* stockpile of cheese!

Calcium—For decades we've been told that we must consume dairy products to get the calcium we need and if we don't get enough, we'll likely get osteoporosis. It turns out that a variety of plants including kale, collard greens, and even chickpeas, have plenty of calcium, and our bodies can absorb the calcium better from many different plants than from dairy. Countries where people drink the most milk, also have the highest rate of osteoporosis! The problem is that the high protein content in cow's milk that helps a calf grow quickly, makes *our* bodies too acidic. To counter the acidity, calcium is pulled from our bones and into our urine. Our bones end up weaker with cow's milk, not stronger. This could be offset by consuming more calcium from dairy or from supplements, or better yet, we could just eat easily absorbable calcium-rich plants.

THE HUMAN BODY

Although most humans do eat meat, we're really not built for it. Physiologically, we don't match up with the carnivore, the herbivore, or even the omnivore as well as we do the *fru*givore—the chimpanzees, apes, and monkeys—whose diet mainly consists of *fru*its, vegetables, and nuts. This is the diet our bodies respond to best and the one we're most physically adapted to. We have flattened molars and a jaw that goes side to side and front and back—great for grinding. Our stomach acid is only moderately acidic—not like a carnivore's that can dissolve tissue. And our intestine is long—nine times our body length. It takes 12-18 hours to completely digest the fiber in our food compared to the much shorter intestine of a carnivore. Their short digestion time is just a few hours so that possible rotted meat goes through their system quickly. We are frugivores. We would be so much healthier and less obese if—like other animals—we simply ate the foods our bodies are designed to eat.

HEALING THE ANIMALS

If we could live happy and healthy lives without harming others...why wouldn't we?

~Edgar's Mission Farm Sanctuary, Australia

While visiting with my parents in cattle-friendly Colorado in January of 2000, we watched the movie *Babe,* about a young pig who is adopted by a border collie and learns how to herd sheep. The movie showed the similarity between pigs and dogs and raised the question of why we consider one to be food and the other a beloved pet. I thought of my own canine companion and certainly wouldn't dream of eating her, so at that moment, sitting 15 miles from some of the largest beef feedlots in the US, I decided to become a vegetarian. I thought I was being kind to animals and not causing them to suffer by not eating them—just their products of milk and eggs. I couldn't have been more wrong.

COWS

The dairy industry has done a fantastic job of suggesting that all dairy products come from happy cows grazing contentedly in bucolic meadows. I went along with this idea for most of my life mainly because I didn't *want* to believe otherwise. But I learned that ignoring the truth about dairy was not only harmful to my own health, but to the cows and to the planet as well. And although there *are* small family farms out there who treat their animals well before slaughtering them, factory farms now provide 99 percent of the country's meat, dairy, and eggs.

Cows are mammals. The females give milk to feed their babies—just like us. In fact, cows are pregnant with their babies for nine months—just like us. The bond between a mother and her baby is one of the strongest in nature. But after a dairy cow gives birth, instead of allowing the mother to nurse and care for her baby, the calf is taken away and the mother's milk is sold to us.

There are two basic kinds of cows—bonier dairy cows and more muscled beef cows. A bony male dairy calf, since he'll never produce milk, has no future and becomes veal within 1-24 weeks of age.

CHICKENS

Like the two types of cows, some chickens are bred to be good egg-layers and lay eggs for 18 months before they're killed when their production slows. Some are good eating chickens or broilers who have more plentiful and tender meat and they're killed when they're just six weeks old. Nine billion chickens are raised for slaughter in the US each year.

FISH

Science and technology have enabled the fishing industry to become so good at catching fish that the oceans could actually be empty by 2048 if we continue fishing at our current rate. Many of us are able to mentally justify eating fish, but are we also okay knowing that countless sea turtles, sharks, dolphins, whales, and even albatross were also killed in order to obtain our fish? Is it worth it? And although the farmed fish industry doesn't kill bycatch, their fish do suffer from overcrowding, disease, and cannibalism. At least in the vegetable gardens, giant zucchinis haven't resorted to that!

HEALING THE ENVIRONMENT

We are, quite literally, gambling with the future of our planet—for the sake of hamburgers.

~Pete Singer

If you're stuck in traffic, on your way home from picking up a cheeseburger, and you're upset at the truck in front of you that's spewing fumes, actually, it's not the truck that's doing most of the polluting—it's your burger.

How? Cows and their manure emit methane and nitrous oxide which are far more powerful than carbon dioxide in heating up the atmosphere. With 1.5 billion cows in the world, it's not surprising that animal agriculture creates more greenhouse gases than all forms of transportation combined.

But it's more than just the gases. Waste from farmed animals is stored in open lagoons, but it doesn't stay there. Much of it seeps out of the lagoons and into the neighboring lands, degrading the soil before reaching the waterways and ending up in our oceans. Algae blooms form from all the excess nitrogen and phosphorous, and the algae sucks up the oxygen in the ocean. Without oxygen, the coral reefs are killed along with the marine life that depends on them and dead zones are created. A quarter of all marine species depend on coral reefs, as well as millions of people around the world. We've already lost half our reefs in the past 30 years due in part to farmed animals and we could lose the rest in the next 30.

We've also lost 20 percent of the Amazon Rainforest—the size of California—for cows. An average of 2.4 acres are being cleared and burned every *minute* by various groups, including companies who have subsidiaries in the US. Instead of having lush trees that give us oxygen, absorb carbon dioxide, and *reduce* greenhouse gases, smoke from the fires, the cows' methane, and nitrous oxide from their waste *add* greenhouse gases. There are about three million different species of plants and animals that live in the Amazon—one tenth of all species in the world—that are threatened by these fires, as well as one million indigenous people who call the Amazon home.

In 1.5 acres, we can produce either 375 pounds of beef or 37,000 pounds of plant-based food. In the US, the livestock industry uses almost *half* the land in the contiguous US, along with 55 percent of our fresh water. It only takes 39 gallons of water to grow a pound of vegetables, but 1850 gallons to produce one pound of beef. We're wastefully growing food to feed our food while millions of Americans are going hungry.

CONNECTIONS AND CHOICES

You must be the change you wish to see in the world.

-Attributed to Mahatma Gandhi

Life can be overwhelming at times and leave us feeling hopeless and helpless. Many turn to food for comfort, but in that food we can also find the power to make choices and restore our hope. To fight COVID-19, we can strengthen our immune systems by eating healthy, whole, plant-based foods. To address global warming today and help save the planet for future generations, we can *also* eat that plant-based diet by keeping those gassy, polluting cows off our plates. To help address racial inequality, we can frequent minority-owned vegan restaurants and shops. To add more compassion and empathy to our world, we can keep the violence off our plates. And to support and encourage our political beliefs and ideals, we can, of course, vote!

Lastly, if you're considering adding more plants and reducing the meat and dairy on *your* plate, here are some helpful tips:

- Try substituting some of the vegan meat, fish, eggs, and dairy alternatives in your regular dishes, including discovering your favorite non-dairy milk.
- Make a complete switch to plant-based or go gradually. Just know that it will take longer to see impressive health benefits when transitioning slowly.
- Embrace the enormous variety of plant-based foods and try new and interesting fruits, vegetables, and grains. Go online and learn how to prepare these new foods and other healthy dishes among the many vegan recipes available.

- Try some vegan dishes in different ethnic cuisines including Thai, South Indian, Ethiopian, and Mediterranean. Mexican and Italian have many options too— simply avoid the meat and cheese.
- Seek out support, and know you're definitely not alone!
  - Check out free programs to help you go vegan including the Physicians Committee for Responsible Medicine's *PCRM's 21-Day Kickstart* and Vegan Outreach's *10 Weeks to Vegan*.
  - Join a plant-based Meetup in your area.
  - Explore the many vegan and plant-based groups on Facebook.
  - Consider trying a plant-based cooking class.
  - Get your dog to join you, as dogs thrive on a vegan diet!

No matter how you decide to go forward, know that now you have the power to make informed choices. And just by going as vegan as you can, your body, the animals, and the whole world will thank you!

Donna Reynolds is a copyeditor, proofreader, gardener, and dog lover, but most of all, she is a vegan. She is grateful to the publishers of this book for the opportunity to inform readers of the life-changing choices they have at every meal and hopes many will discover how much they, the animals, and the world will benefit from putting more plants on their plates!

The Healing

Rena Robinett

Sereana wasn't as spry as usual. She moved around the cottage with a tired, listless air, while humming to herself. She was a small plain creature, but her square face and form spoke out: *You must spit in the eyes of your enemies and laugh at what befalls you, it may look like a short journey on a long road but at the end of the line it's the beginning of another circle.*

The long red skirt that hung to her ankles complimented a loose embroidered beige top. Her tiny feet were bare, except for the anklets of silver bells, and she wore a ring on each finger, and a tiny gold ring in the side of her pert nose.

The room fit her like her clothes, comfortable, fluid, and artful. It was a space designed for living, reflection, and joy. A soft gray sofa, a comfy blue chair and matching ottoman, three small wood tables with candles, and walls layered with drawings, paintings, and tapestries arranged in pleasant clutter except for one wall covered with books of every shape, size, color, and dimension. Several leafy plants filled the air with the aroma of fresh herbs—a rosemary bush by the window, young branches of basil and mint sprouting from tiny pots on the counter, along with the peppery fragrance of fennel—joined seamlessly with the vanilla scent of her homemade candles.

With a steaming cup in her hands, she sat on the blue chair looking out the open window taking in the dark blue sky that hung like a wash above the forest at the end of her tidy plot of land. "Something is coming, I can feel it," her voice was raspy, but high-pitched, like a child with a cold. It possessed a gentle lisp, a faint accent of an ancient tongue long forgotten yet with traces of seldom used human speech. Drinking her tea, she tried to form pictures of what she was feeling while vague shapes coalesced around her thoughts. She knew she wouldn't be able to say no to her calling, whatever it was.

As evening fell, she put on her long nightgown and got in her wooden bed with its carved tall pillars. Nestling under her soft jewel colored quilt, she drifted off to sleep. She awoke to a mewling sound and instinctively swung off the bed and moved cautiously to the front door. The mewling grew louder and more recognizable as crying. She opened the front door to a human girl huddled on her door step crying uncontrollably. Extending her arms, she helped the girl stand and ushered her inside.

"Where am I?" The sobs stopped as she looked around the room.

"You are in my house, safe. Let me get you some tea." Sereana went into her kitchen and put on the tea kettle. She pulled down several small jars of herbs and mixed them in two large mugs. Waiting for the water to boil, she peeked through the doorway at the girl. She had dark, spikey bluish hair, big eyes, and a narrow face. She was thin, but didn't look frail.

Sereana carried the steaming mugs into the room, put hers on the table by the sofa, and handed the other to the girl who had taken the blue chair.

"How did you get here?" Sereana asked.

"I don't know. My boyfriend Danny and I were protesting in the city with our friends. We left home even though there is a terrible virus everywhere. We wore masks and gloves and thought we'd be safe." Her hand flew to her mouth as she sobbed.

Sereana reached in her pocket and handed her a large white handkerchief. "Here. What's your name?"

"Tasha," she wiped the tears. "The police came shouting and running after us. That's when, my boyfriend Danny fell." She stopped, then wide-eyed, breathless added, "He got shot in the head and blood was running down his face. People surrounded us and I was screaming and screaming. An ambulance came and took him away. I sat on the ground, wishing and wishing it was all a nightmare and I would wake up soon. I hurt all over and the more I cried the darker it got all around me. Then I looked up and saw you."

Sereana felt sorry for the human. She had heard rumors that Earth was in trouble. Humans weren't usually her concern. There were the "others" the Elonas, who handled that.

"Where exactly is this city you came from?" she said.

"Portland, Oregon." Tasha sniffled.

"Wait here, relax. I'll be right back." Sereana walked across the room and into her bedroom. She undressed and put on a pair of tan pants with loads of pockets, slipped a long, dark blue shirt over her head, pushed up the sleeves, and sat on a chair by her bed to put on a pair of worn lace-up boots. Stomping the boots lightly as she rose, Sereana stood before a mirror to brush her long white hair into a braid at the back of her head.

When she saw that Tasha had fallen asleep on the couch, she went back to her bedroom and gathered some of her most valuable possessions, putting them in her pants' pockets and a cloth bag. A burst of energy took over her being. She had thought her continuous thirst for the next adventure to unfold had abated. She was wrong. The desire to help, generally reserved for reprobates, adventurers, travelers of the stars, and wise solitary women with stray bits of green magic in their blood, had returned. She put the bag next to the back door in the kitchen, and returned to her chair to finish her tea while the girl slept.

Tasha's face was still wet with tears when she awoke. She recalled having the weirdest dream about a funny old lady. But it was a good dream, especially compared to remembering that Danny was gone. She sat up and drew back seeing the old lady from her dream, sitting on the chair across from her.

"You are not dreaming," Sereana said. "We need to get moving."

"Where am I?"

"No worries. We're leaving anyway." She stood and gave a last look around her sweet little abode. "Follow me," she told Tasha. At the back door, Sereana picked up her cloth bag and threw it over her shoulder. They strode through her backyard with its frog water pond and into the forest, where they both faded into the darkness.

When they came up towards a bright light above their heads, Sereana looked around trying to figure out exactly where they were. She pulled a tiny bottle from one of her pockets, popped off the cork, and a little something flew out and around her head. "Come on, Tasha," she patted Tasha on the back. "She will guide us." She grabbed Tasha's hand and they followed the flutter of wings.

They arrived in the city of Portland, Oregon, in a country named USA. The streets were quiet. No people. No sounds. Something felt wrong to Sereana. She hadn't been on

Earth since what humans called the 60's. It was bad then, but under the badness there was a thread of wonderfulness. There was no wonderfulness where they stood. The air tasted like Europe during the Black Plague.

Noticing in the distance a crowd of people jammed together in a variety of costumes and gear, they walked towards them. Folks were milling around and chanting. Gently pushing through the crowd Sereana and Tasha came to the front of the line and found a solid wall of women in orange shirts called 'the moms.' On the side of the line were 'the dads' armed with leaf blowers and an odd assortment of yard tools. "Oh, no," Sereana, even sensing danger, couldn't help but chuckle. "What have these humans got themselves into now?" It all seemed ridiculous, but underneath the comedy del arte, she identified an old familiar taste and smell. It made her skin crawl up and down her spine. Her eyes filled with tears. This was bad, really bad. A flash of ancient recollections came to her along with the image of a split tail and glowing eyes. He was back. Lost in thought, she didn't realize what was happening until she heard Tasha cry out, and watched as the people around them pushed them and shouted to get out of the way.

Big men in helmets, armed with guns and riot batons were charging toward the pro-testers demanding that they all move away from the building they were facing. They were pushing, gassing, and shooting at the moms. It was an evil she had seen before but had not expected to see again. She moved with the crowd, slowly working her way to the side-lines but had lost sight of Tasha.

Sitting hidden by the side of the building, Sereana pulled from one of her pockets an old piece of bone, and from her bag a feather and some dust from an ancient grave. She began muttering under her breath. She needed to stop the demon controlling these opposing forces. It was a risk she was willing to take and she muttered faster and louder barely notice-able in the chaos. She placed the bone on the ground, sprinkled the dust over it and began waving the feather through the air, around her head, shoulders, knees and feet. She chanted louder and louder, as a fog enveloped her. She switched the feather from hand to hand and pointed it at the big men nearest her and their rifles melted away, followed by the helmets, vests, ammo, goggles, boots, pants, flak jackets, brown shirts and pants. She waved and pointed at the big men further and further out, and they were also stripped of all their clothes and gear. They howled in shock, cowering and using their hands to cover themselves. The big men chased by the crowd of laughing people ran into the building.

One big man, who had not been stripped of his clothing, could see her through the fog and was coming fast in her direction. He pulled his weapon ready to shoot, but she waved her feather and shouted another ancient chant. The earth under him rose in an undulating wave of concrete and he tumbled to the ground. By the time he stood and jumped up looking for her, she had vanished.

Sereana found Tasha sitting on a deserted sidewalk and sat next to her. "So glad to see you," she said. "From now on I will keep you by my side, and I promise to teach you many of my ways." Then she added, "The demon is back on Earth but with your help we can help humanity." If Tasha was surprised by the statement, it didn't show.

That evening Sereana and Tasha headed back to downtown Portland and joined the protesters. Sereana held a tiny rock, and when she brought her hand up everyone around her was encircled in a radiant aura. Everyone except the big men in riot gear and others that had infiltrated the peaceful protesters, to cause mayhem.

Once again, the men in riot gear were stripped naked. Guns melted at their feet, along with their hats, masks, shirts, bullets, belts, batons, pants, and shoes. The violent people causing the chaos were also stripped of all their clothing. They stood with their mouths open, speechless. Sereana looked swiftly around for the demon, but he was nowhere in sight. "I will get him," she murmured to herself.

For the next few weeks, Sereana and Tasha worked their way across the country going from one demonstration to another until a kid on TikTok posted a photo of Sereana, "I think this old granny is able to see evil and she's zapping them naked." Evidently, he had attended a demonstration in Florida and caught her in action.

Sereana and Tasha reached Washington D.C., people were in the streets everywhere, and most sat in emulation of Gandhi. More and more people were saying, "Violence is not the answer, we must work together for peace and understanding."

The people that had been stripped of everything tried to put on some kind of clothing, but it wouldn't stay on. They could do nothing but stay home.

The nasty large man who had started all this chaos, and who Sereana was positive to be closely aligned with the demon she had confronted on the streets of Portland, Oregon was holed up in the white house.

The crowd began shouting the large man's name while they pushed forward toward the barricade surrounding the house that wasn't his. Whispers wafted through the huge gathering, "He's coming out!" Sereana and Tasha moved to the front of the crowd, until they stood in front of the barricade. There he was, standing on the steps gesturing with his stubby arms and tiny hands. Sereana smiled as she took the feather from her bag and held it up. She looked forward to this one.

The young people in the crowd created a large circle around her as they whispered, "It's her! It's the granny!" She did her chant, and as expected, the men and women around the large man and the large man himself were stark-naked. They began to wail, especially the large man who used his tiny hands to cover his tiny private part. He yelled for someone to stand in front of him but no one was paying any attention. They stood stunned and naked on the steps of the house that wasn't theirs.

The people tore down the barricades and entered the house that they belonged in. Then, they called in those they trusted to get on with the business of running the country and helping the world. Everyone would be fed, and housed, and given jobs with good pay. There would be excellent medical care, and the children and elders would be cared for, and education would be free. It was an amazing, astonishing time of cooperation, discovery, and love. People from all over the world came together in groups and gatherings to develop new ways to live better with the earth, all it's creatures, and each other.

This happened everywhere in the world, from Buckingham Palace, where the Queen was stripped naked along with some of the Parliament members, to the Kremlin where Putin tried to strangle every naked person around him.

All naked folks were sent to the Amazon Forest in South America, to be interred much like they wanted to inter everyone else in the world. And the men and woman were separated so that they couldn't breed. If any of them showed signs of becoming good people, which some believed was possible, they would be allowed back into society.

It was also decided that anyone worth over one billion dollars would donate anything over that amount to help repair the Earth. Everyone agreed except for one greedy man. He ended up naked, for the rest of his life.

Sereana was ready to go home. She missed her little cottage among the stars. When she informed Tasha she would be leaving the next morning, she also told of her connection with other beings called Elonas. They, who like her belonged in another Universe, would be keeping an eye on things.

Sereana's phone rang that evening. "Sereana," Tasha said. "We are gathered at Angkor Wat and we need you to come as soon as possible."

"Why? What's happening?" she sighed.

"No idea. But it's urgent, very urgent that you come right now, please," Tasha said.

Sereana twirled around and around until she found herself standing at the top of a 500-foot-high temple in the center of a forest in

Cambodia. The large wide chamber, the steps up to the temple and the surrounding Angkor Wat fields below were covered with Elonas and people of all races. Everyone was dressed colorfully, carrying balloons and kites and paper umbrellas, laughing, and talking, chanting, and singing. Sereana smiled, when she saw Tasha walking towards her. "We couldn't let you go home without saying thank you," Tasha said.

And they did. They said "mahalo" to each other for saving themselves, each other, and the world.

Rena Robinett currently has eight short stories published in various magazines, ezines, and anthologies with international and national publications; and has self-published one Science Fiction novelette, BREED. She has had an adventurous life, traveling the world and then living in Hawaii. for several decades. She now resides in Northern California, working at a modern art museum. Rena has a BA in English Composition from California State at Fresno and has attended, by invitation, the Iowa Writer's Workshop summer session and the Napa Valley Writers Workshop. Rena is currently working on a memoir in two parts and a short story collection.

WE. RISE.

Kim Conrad

It is time for the souls of the world to unite
   in song
To wake from the dead of sleep long induced
By those who have not wanted the Universe
To Awaken To Itself
And Sing
In Harmony
In Balance for All Things
Living from
The Heart beating Nucleus of the Cosmos,
Sparking Life in Every Cell.
It beckons each of us,
"Listen to me...
Listen to me!
THIS IS the time
That You came FOR
THIS IS the time
That You came TO

Stand Strong,
Stand Upright
and
Speak with Carefully Crafted,
Powerfully Integrating,
Alliance Calling Wisdom.
Become Comfortable with being
    uncomfortable.
Walk together.
Listen.
Reframe, Relearn, Revise
And Optimize
RISING FROM
THE HEART SPEAKING
DEPTHS OF YOUR SOUL
THEN NOTHING CAN STOP YOU."

Having Nothing to Say
Speaks volumes of complicit acquiescence
And gives entitlement to destructive powers
Constructed from years of amassed
    insecurities,
Obedience, at all costs, to pains protections
And fabricated lack of self-worth.
These individuals are no longer able to
    value life
Other than their own and like-minded
    patrons,
Because it would mean

Having to face the pain of
Their abandoned and repressed omissions.

Silence is now Violence.
Staying 'safe in silence' is
No longer 'staying safe'.
You came to be Heard
NOT herded.
The only wrong thing to say is Nothing.

Let go of false conditioned fears
And head-tripping 'shoulditis'
That protected you from blooming
In your magnificence.
RISE FROM
THE DEPTHS OF YOUR SOUL
That unquestionable knowing of the Cosmos
Pulsing through every fiber of your being.
Listen.
Reframe, Relearn, Revise
AND OPTIMIZE TOGETHER.
THEN NOTHING CAN STOP YOU.
THEN NOTHING CAN STOP US.
WE. RISE.

Like the Phoenix from the ashes.
Like the Butterfly from the caterpillar.
WE. RISE.

Avalanche

Do not despair
When all about you
Chaos reigns.
It is often the avalanche
That uncovers lost cities;
The whispers of marinating
Treasures waiting until
It was time to see the
Light of day again.

Uncover your hearts
Lay bare your souls
Love that which has
Felt lost, mistreated
Or lonely.
Let your DNA unravel
Into kingdoms and queendoms
Waiting to be born.
Tuck yourself into
Your heart again.
It's time.

Shine like stars
Because. You. Are. One.
Let waters cleanse
Generations of old

Stories whose time has
Come to fall away like
Petals on a dying rose
That gives birth to new seeds.

Use your being's
Universally Given
Truth seeking voice to be
The Eye of the Storm.
Stand and speak out
Re-Source-Fully
Peacefully,
Powerfully,
Poignantly,
Unceasingly
For IN – Justice.
Use Laced Arrows
To Pierce False Foundations
With the Accuracy
Of Unified Intention.
Stand For
Your fellow man and woman,
For All of Life and Planet.
Unite In This Calling
Of The Universe.

There are cells who came
To dissolve the caterpillar

And
There are Those –
US
Who came to
Create the Butterfly.
Imaginal Cellular listening
That births from beyond
All conditioned knowledge
To the pages of
The Book
Future Written
Whose Time Is Now
Co-Creating This Butterfly
Destined In It's BE-Coming
Through action taking
Imaginal Cells Marching Our
Keenly Awarenessing
Collaborating
Resiliencing
Integrating
Future Forward.

The Stakes are High.
Our Future Here
Affects the Future of
The Entire Solar System
We Are Part Of.
Silence is Not Golden

(*unless* you're meditating)
Use quiet reflection
To give clarified voice
So knowing is clear, effective
And alignment making for All.
Life needs to unravel
To Reweave itself.
We are part of life's
Re-WEavers.
Uncomfortable though
It may be on the edge
Of creation's brilliance,
TRUST
In the innate IN-Tell-I-gence
Of Life itself.
Internal Growth
Does not happen
Unless there is a choice
To meet the challenge.
Greatness is forged
Through meeting
Great challenges.

EVEN IF you be
Shaky and Doubting
Or Ready and Willing
Or Both
BEgin.

Make calls
Volunteer again
Write
Learn
STRETCH
Keep going
Receive
Help Others
March
Breathe
Vote
BE Kind To You and This World
Have the 'Soulular' window cleaner
Wash clean the windows of your soul.

BE. CAUSE.
Because You. Are. Designed. To.
Because We. Are. Designed. To.
In This Together
We Are.

I See the Perfection In You.
Please Look In The Mirror.

Kim Conrad is an award-winning and best-selling author, re-markable intuitive, and has been called a gifted 'Interior De-signer' that guides you to create the life you love to live. She is a dynamic and inspiring example of what it's like to make it through anything. Having rebuilt her body and her life three times, spoken with over a million people in her 35+

years of business and guided thousands she combines her Masters in Psychology, Reiki mastership, performance background and sense of humor to make her coaching, workshops and presentations fun and life-enhancing at the same time. She has been called a 'pioneer of language' and her voice a 'healing medicine'. She has also hit a golf ball backwards. KimConrad.com / Facebook.com/KimConradVisionary / YouTube: rebrand.ly/iak6zom

We All Deserve Better

Keith Manuel

These are tumultuous times. Division around the world is exploding when we should be creating solutions together. Nationalism, religious extremism, wars, COVID-19 and rising fascism all deserve our attention, but pale in comparison to climate crisis. The climate emergency we now face is the largest challenge in human history. Can we overcome it by making drastic changes to our paradigm of 'societal norms' and simultaneously move to 100% renewable energy on this planet? What about eliminating wars, dictators, corrupt governments and so much hate? Can we accomplish all of this and end up with nutritious food, clean water, healthcare, shelter, and jobs available for everyone on our planet? I believe we can. My book "A

Revolutionary Solution," available without cost, offers hope and solutions so humans and other species on earth not only survive but flourish.

Much of this environmental crisis can be linked to money—facilitating accumulation and consolidation of wealth by some to the detriment of others. When profit rules motivation, our environment isn't a consideration. Eleven percent starve worldwide while production yields enough for 130% of our people[1]. Fossil fuels burn while current technology exists for 100% renewables worldwide[2,3]. Our workforce can increase 44% without increasing the population[4,5]. The problems caused by money are endless: from crime, war, and famine to telemarketers, litigation and loan sharks. Much of our pollution is driven by the desire for easy profits such as inferior materials and workmanship, cutting costs by ignoring environmental laws, or lobbying to lower or remove them. I propose we will *thrive* by removing money—all monetary systems worldwide. The human resource savings would be over 22% (USA) from job eliminations include financial institutions, insurance companies, stock markets, patent/copyright, law firms, and many more. A drastic increase in our workforce to fight global warming can build that much needed infrastructure. Greed, wealth accumulation and resource depletion, advances global warming and other problems, as do the imaginary lines we draw to signify national borders.

Roughly 200 nations must make radical changes to stop climate change. Without a consensus, individual nations continue to create and amplify division that shape wars and create enormous environmental impacts. A reasonable timeline to save our environment will only materialize by accepting new paradigms for humanity—without nations, wars, military buildup, nuclear threat or germ warfare stockpiles. Let's explore a future in 2040, without money or nations.

SOCIETY RE-ENVISIONED

A typically work week is 25 to 30 hours. After the flood of job training and retraining in the first year, everyone now works for common goals instead of personal wealth. Those few opposed to our social norms headed for the wilderness to hide or 'survive in nature'. Others went to multi-million-dollar bunkers and mega-yachts in frantic attempts to protect 'wealth'. A few individuals and small remote villages don't participate in our society, but they possess no known weapons or munitions caches and their negligible numbers continue to dwindle. Historically long, tiring, low wage jobs are gone, along with those trying to "get ahead". Everyone understands when we all contribute; we all get ahead. A large contingency still provides extra work-hours toward cures for disease, solutions on infrastructure, pollution, and environmental cleanup. Careers seeming important twenty years ago are now replaced with projects assisting our fellow inhabitants and the planet. Many formerly in the military worked bringing infrastructure, including roads, electricity, water, and sewer systems to areas underserved. Food, healthcare and assistance with self-sufficiencies followed.

People with physical or mental barriers, including retirees, are not required to contribute workhours, though many find fulfilling ways to assist society. Our sophisticated communication, transportation and energy grids ensure needs are accessible to everyone at all times. Resolving food, shelter, clothing and healthcare insecurities increased our already expanded global workforce by another 22%—almost a billion new workers[6], no longer spending all day seeking food, shelter and other necessities. These citizens, now free to create, participate, and contribute and are some of our most dedicated workers. Innovations have skyrocketed around the world overnight as hope flourished.

Most dangerous and repetitive jobs are now performed by robotics[7] and, together with other advances, replaced 25% of jobs formerly performed by humans and should double within 15 years[8]. Many scientists and former military personnel work perfecting defense against stray asteroids, comets, and rogue planets.

Musicians, actors, painters, sculptors, dancers, and other artists now have more free time to create. Arts, encouraged and supported, are an important part of our lives. Though still fighting a global crisis, humanity's expressive art has stayed vibrant! Most enjoy significantly more leisure time than in 2020 when slave wages and political chaos ruled.

Private car ownership is obsolete as technologies existing since 2018 were leveraged[9,10,11]. Personal maintenance, driving and storing also disappeared. Vehicles no longer sit in disuse and disrepair, saving raw materials and production time. They operate from centralized storage, maintenance and charging locations, always well maintained and adjusted for weather. Stranded vehicles, injured motorists and traffic congestion also disappeared. With independent navigation and global transportation communication, collisions are nearly extinct. Deaths or maiming by drunk drivers, distracted teens, and long-haul truckers falling asleep from driving too many hours supporting their family also ceased. We all use a simple transportation system, communicating needs from a phone or public kiosk, with pickup time, location, and cargo needs. Priority is always given to urgent/emergency needs.

Prisons are largely gone, as removing money and power incentives deterred most criminal activity. Most former prisoners were successfully treated for mental health issues, addressing root problems instead of punishing symptoms. A small number remain, for whom treatment is ineffective, or are deemed a danger instead of asset to society. People capable but unwilling to contribute work-hours are typically reassigned to least desirable, high demand jobs. Refusal to contribute leaves no reciprocal incentive from society, so they will often experience longer wait times for vehicles, lower quality groceries, and no vacations (currently two months per year). Their alternative also includes basic jail time; typically the first and only step needed. Those originally skeptical about society's ability to incentivize the 'unwilling to participate', when everyone's basic needs are 'taken care of' are now convinced. Few actually need incentives, as desiring to contribute is human nature, up there with survival. Instead of a world heading directly into disaster, we are now 9 billion humans with common goals.

For everyone to work together,
everyone needs to work, together!

Hurricanes, typhoons and tornadoes have continued increasing in number, strength and destruction, and will likely continue 10–20 years before decreasing. As drought and wildfires escalated, along with their impacts, other areas faced storms and flooding. Many coastal communities vanished or relocated, and efforts continue to protect and relocate populations. Methane released from warming tundra fields formerly frozen for centuries increased global warming faster than predicted. Additionally, increased absorption of solar energy near both poles from massive losses of snow and sea ice heightened our struggle. Each setback only increased our resolve to fight global warming, and we are *winning*.

One example is in plastics. Innovations include micro plastics-eating bacteria, developed in 2017[12], which reduced concentrations and damage to marine life substantially. Virgin plastics production is replaced with plant-based biodegradable 'plastics' and recycled plastics. Work continues to create '2nd stage' rocket fuel from plastic waste. Reusable electric first-stage rockets to propel them safely from our atmosphere. After separation the 2nd stage plastic fuel and cargo will continue sunward[13].

Major victories in soil conservation and restoration by eliminating harmful farming practices such as chemical fertilizers, pesticides and herbicides mean organic food grown with sustainable farming practices worldwide. Soil health improvements created major improvements to stream, river and groundwater pollution. Devastating effects of farming meat, from antibiotic overload to increased disease and runoff halted. Instead of burning forests for grazing, we replant forests, replenishing soil and increasing the health of our water and us all. Meat is still consumed, from herd thinning or pest control. Few consume meat though, as its negative effects on health are common knowledge.

New and previously undiscovered disease outbreaks increased as habitats expanded for rats, ticks and mosquitos. Thawing glaciers and tundra frozen for millennia continue to release more diseases, pathogens, and methane. Fortunately, infectious diseases are now faced globally with faster pathogen isolation, cures and vaccines. Our pandemic protection is better than any individual countries once had.

In all tasks, the most qualified are sought to participate in the field and often serve as expert "decision-makers". Decision-makers make up our government, managing neighborhood to global issues and solutions, planning and progress. Every issue or threat is an opportunity for hope for our future and love for each other.

We are not surviving, we are flourishing.

Improved quality of products and services continues as job skill, satisfaction and happiness increases quality for everyone. Without corporate secrets, copyrights or patents, we *all* use the best formulas, processes and designs, and make constant improvements shared globally. Although humans possess instinctual "fight or flight" and are easily corrupted by greed, our basic instincts of love, contributing our share, and personal fortitude have towered above.

Some originally quite wealth resisted, although many felt relief no longer trapped by their money. Interestingly, more resistance came from those living on poverty's edge, fearing a world with everyone fed, clothed and housed would mean even less for them. As word grew of a potential world with such improved quality of life for everyone *and* reversing climate change, hope grew. Love grew and blossomed as our hopes became reality.

Though many years remain to completely stop and reverse climate change we have accomplished much already. Lead climatologists agree climate change reversal is realistic.

One hundred percent renewable energy resources, sustainable farming practices, elimination of farmed fish, birds and mammals, and a moratorium on plastics manufacturing are making huge impacts, curbing the largest climate change contributors. Plastic waste, poor quality work and disorganized supply chains are gone. We all fight for our survival together, with innovation cultivated for public good instead of personal advantage.

Another huge advantage removing monetary systems was the volumes of 'laws' no longer needed, in addition to lawyers, courts, and staff. Community Standards (sort of a working set of rules for all) guarantee equality for everyone. Additionally, they include rights to nutritious food, clean water, appropriate shelter, religious freedoms and the right to choose your own path in life.

Education and knowledge have grown significantly, as have skills. Without old fears, suppression and misdirection we now realize we *can* all live, love, and *thrive* together, working toward common goals. Within a generation, life in 2020 was unrecognizable.

Innovation, best found in well-nourished and nurtured minds, has been staggering in number with new freedoms and equality. Without striations of social class or corporate and national secrets we all have equal access to any information and education.

The internet is the valuable tool and gift to society its creators and early adopters envisioned. Without marketing and advertising, data theft, or moneymaking schemes what remains is society's monumental wealth of information and knowledge, with useful search engine results instead of deceptive marketing and sales promotions.

You may wonder how government operates. How we survive the draw of power, greed and corruption. Our government takes the best aspects of true social democracy, but with a huge number of diverse decision-makers. Additionally, every citizen has rights of redress on any decision. Instead of closed-door backroom deals and negotiations, legislation and proposed legislation is publicly available. Without incentives for illegal, unjust and deceptive deals, all governing activity is fully transparent. Citizens showing an aptitude for good decision making and who desire serving in that capacity can apply for Level 1 decision-maker, voted on by neighborhood peers. From there they are slowly and purposefully promoted, voted out, or asked to remain at that level. Nobody is promoted beyond their comfort level.

Level 1 decision-makers handle neighborhood issues, including shared resources, localized weather events, and nonviolent personal conflicts. Instead of working independently, they work in groups of three helping ensure fair decisions, different viewpoints, and no ties. Redress is always heard by next higher-level decision-makers. Level 2 decision-makers have groups of five managing communities, typically 10 to 30 neighborhoods. Duties include community supply and demand, infrastructure and construction projects, and Level 1 promotions. Level 2-4 decisions require 'redress petitions' signed by 3% of their populations. Level 3 folks primarily deal with larger regional issues environmental strategies, regional supply and demand, and ensuring citizens' rights. Coordinating with Level 4 and Level 5 decision-makers these 51 member groups are the lowest level decision-makers to hear, judge and "pass sentence" on violations of community standards. Sentences previously involving court fines, jail and even corporal punishment are gone, excepting rare jail time decisions reserved for violent/repeat offenders unresponsive to mental health care or standard incentives.

Level 4 decision-makers, somewhat like old Parliament or Congress in their scope, have groups of 1001. Their primary focus is managing infrastructure and resources on larger scales than Level 3s.

Level 5 decision-makers, the very top level that exists and comprised of a diverse cross-section of people from every region and ethnicity, manage internal and external global issues. With full access to *all* knowledge, they hold the responsibility to shield humanity from information too destructive and dangerous for the general population. Level 5 decision-makers are something like the old United Nations delegation, but with actual power for global change.

Housing for everyone had challenges, but vacant housing, office space, and newly vacant buildings formerly housing banks, insurance companies, investment advisors, etc. provided short-term housing for many. Some required migration, and these vacated properties had deconstruction teams removing raw materials for re-use. Everywhere adjustments were made ensuring equality in shelter. Larger families needing room moved to larger accommodations, freeing up smaller abodes. Former owners of estates and mansions moved or were required to share the property. While everyone had shelter, disparities existed in early years, especially regarding furnishings. Many former mansions are now centers for education, orphanages, athletic centers and vacation spots. Looking back, I am amazed at the difficulty some had letting go of material objects.

I experienced pure joy as former divisions of classes disappeared, along with so much hate. Without distribution and manufacture harmful drug use has dried up, and excellent treatment centers are plentiful. Subsequently crimes like petty larceny, grand theft and armed robberies all essentially disappeared. Rehabilitation and lack of poverty, peer pressure and racism were key. From neighborhoods up the entire world works together and looks out for each other. In our darkest hour, the lantern of hope directed us to the light of love. We replaced hate, greed, jealousy, cholera, famine and walls with hope, freedom, love, health, peace and community.

Thank you for taking your valuable time to hear my solutions. Too utopian? Ask yourself why you don't deserve the best. You do! This will not be easy, but nothing worth getting ever is: real democracy, equal rights for *everyone*, no wars, famine, dictators or nuclear weapons and jails mostly empty repurposed for emergency evacuation housing. Can you imagine a world without borders, politics, corporations, money problems and so much hate? I have! Visit ARevolutionarySolution.com for the most up-to-date information, my complimentary book, and discover how you can create this future!

Future generations ALL depend on us.

Notes:

1. Eric Holt-Gimenez, "We Already Grow Enough Food For 10 Billion People -- and Still Can't End Hunger: Hunger is caused by poverty and inequality, not scarcity. For the past two decades, the rate of global food production has increased faster than the rate of global population growth," *Huffington Post*, May 02, 2012, https://www.huffpost.com/entry/world-hunger_b_1463429
2. "Can we supply 100% of our energy needs from renewable sources?" *Credible Carbon*, Accessed November 19, 2018, https://www.crediblecarbon.com/news-and-info/news/can-we-supply-100-of-our-energy-needs-from-renewable-sources/.

3. Mark Z. Jacobson, "Transition to 100 Percent Wind, Water, and Solar (video)," *American Association for the Advancement of Science (AAAS)*, Accessed November 19, 2018, https://www.eurekalert.org/multimedia/pub/148263.php.

4. Keith Manuel, *A Revolutionary Solution*, (Portland, OR: A Revolutionary Solution, 2020), pp19.

5. "Employment-to-population ratio," *Wikipedia*, Accessed December 10, 2018, https://en.wikipedia.org/wiki/Employment-to-population_ratio.

6. Keith Manuel, *A Revolutionary Solution*.

7. Rob Marvin, "Robots May Replace A Lot More Human Jobs By 2022," *PC Magazine*, September 24, 2018, https://uk.pcmag.com/why-axis/117550/robots-may-replace-a-lot-more-human-jobs-by-2022.

8. Rob Marvin, "Robots May Replace A Lot More Human Jobs By 2022".

9. "New mobility is here: Autonomous, shared and electric," *Navya*, Accessed December 12, 2018, http://navya.tech/en/.

10. Julia Pyper, "The Key to Autonomous Electric Vehicles Takes Another Step Toward Commercialization: Nissan partners with industry pioneer WiTricity to create a global wireless charging ecosystem," *Greentech Media*, February 09, 2017, https://www.greentechmedia.com/articles/read/the-key-to-autonomous-electric-transportation-takes-another-step-toward-com.

11. "46 Corporations Working On Autonomous Vehicles," *CB Insights*, September 4, 2018, https://www.cbinsights.com/research/autonomous-driverless-vehicles-corporations-list/.

12. Deborah Netburn, "Newly discovered bacteria can eat plastic bottles," *Los Angeles Times*, March 11, 2016, https://phys.org/news/2016-03-newly-bacteria-plastic-bottles.html.

13. "Hybrid-propellant rocket," *Wikipedia*, Accessed November 17, 2018, https://en.wikipedia.org/wiki/Hybrid-propellant_rocket.

"46 Corporations Working On Autonomous Vehicles." *CB Insights*. September 4, 2018.

https://www.cbinsights.com/research/autonomous-driverless-vehicles-corporations-list/.

"Can we supply 100% of our energy needs from renewable sources?" *Credible Carbon*. Accessed November 19, 2018. https://www.crediblecarbon.com/news-and-info/news/can-we-supply-100-of-our-energy-needs-from-renewable-sources/.

"Employment-to-population ratio." *Wikipedia*. Accessed December 10, 2018. https://en.wikipedia.org/wiki/Employment-to-population_ratio.

Holt-Gimenez, Eric. "We Already Grow Enough Food For 10 Billion People -- and Still Can't End Hunger: Hunger is caused by poverty and inequality, not scarcity. For the past two decades, the rate of global food production has increased faster than the rate of global population growth." *Huffington Post*. May 02, 2012. https://www.huffpost.com/entry/world-hunger_b_1463429.

"Hybrid-propellant rocket." *Wikipedia*. Accessed November 17, 2018. https://en.wikipedia.org/wiki/Hybrid-propellant_rocket.

Jacobson, Mark Z. "Transition to 100 Percent Wind, Water, and Solar (video)." *American Association for the Advancement of Science (AAAS)*. Accessed November 19, 2018. https://www.eurekalert.org/multimedia/pub/148263.php.

Manuel, Keith. *A Revolutionary Solution*. Portland, OR: A Revolutionary Solution. 2020.

Marvin, Rob. "Robots May Replace A Lot More Human Jobs By 2022." *PC Magazine*. September 24, 2018. https://uk.pcmag.com/why-axis/117550/robots-may-replace-a-lot-more-human-jobs-by-2022.

Netburn, Deborah. "Newly discovered bacteria can eat plastic bottles." *Los Angeles Times*. March 11, 2016. https://phys.org/news/2016-03-newly-bacteria-plastic-bottles.html.

"New mobility is here: Autonomous, shared and electric." *Navya*. Accessed December 12, 2018. http://navya.tech/en/.

Pyper, Julia. "The Key to Autonomous Electric Vehicles Takes Another Step Toward Commercialization: Nissan partners with industry pioneer WiTricity to create a global wireless charging ecosystem." *Greentech Media.* February 09, 2017. https://www.greentechmedia.com/articles/read/the-key-to-autonomous-electric-transportation-takes-another-step-toward-com.

Keith Manuel, a former chef, small business owner and software designer is the author of "A Revolutionary Solution". His book results from many years of research and interviews into ways to feed and house the world. Prior to focusing on global solutions, he worked on local small business and charity organization solutions. A budding author, Keith has published short works on Daily Kos for many years. Diving into new careers is nothing new; he became an international award-winning ice sculptor within a year of his initiation. Keith lives in the Pacific Northwest with his wife, dog, and vegetable garden.

Made in the USA
Las Vegas, NV
11 January 2021

15717530R00101